Portuguese Africa and the West

WILLIAM MINTER

Portuguese Africa and the West

Monthly Review Press
New York and London

The photo on the jacket is of an MPLA
detachment on the Benguela Railroad.

Library of Congress Cataloging in Publication Data
Minter, William, 1942-
    Portuguese Africa and the West.
    Bibliography: p.
    1. Portugal—Colonies—Africa.   2. Portu-
gal—Relations (general) with the United States.
3. United States—Relations (general) with
Portugal.   4. Portugal—Relations (general)
with foreign countries. I. Title.
DT36.M56 1973   325'.3469'096   73-8054
ISBN 0-85345-295-4

Monthly Review Press
116 West 14th Street, New York, N.Y. 10011
33/37 Moreland Street, E.C. 1

First Printing

Manufactured in the United States of America

Contents

5

Contents

List of Maps

Preface

The research for this book began in 1969. The aim was to spell out American complicity in Portugal's colonial wars, to let people know what was going on, and help to make possible mobilization to stop that complicity. It would be pleasant to report that in the time it took in writing and in publication such a book has become unnecessary. It has not. Instead, the December 1971 Azores agreement arranged by the Nixon administration has dramatically increased American support for Portugal.

But the struggle of the African liberation movements goes on. And awareness of that struggle is slowly increasing in the West, including the United States. It is in this context that I would like to dedicate this book, above all to the liberation fighters and the peoples of Angola, Mozambique, and Guinea-Bissau, and then also to those others, many of whom have helped directly or indirectly with this book, who are working within the western countries for solidarity with the oppressed peoples of Southern Africa. It is my hope that this book may make some contribution to that effort.

W.M.

Preface to the American Edition

This book is the same as the British edition with the exception of Chapter 10, which was written in June 1973 to update the earlier chapters and to provide a more detailed analysis of the Nixon policies than was possible before. In its essence, the picture of United States support for Portuguese colonialism remains unchanged; the task of countering that support is no less necessary than before. But, as is shown in Chapter 10, the trend of Nixon policy is not just to continue the previous support, but to increase it. In the black community and among progressive forces in different sectors of American society, the awareness and willingness to act on Southern Africa is growing. That growth must continue if any serious impact is to be made in removing the weight being thrown by United States government and business against African struggles for liberation.

W.M.

Note: Since the British edition of this book was written the name of Congo (Kinshasa) has been changed to Zaire. In the text, the name used is that current at the time of the events being discussed.

1 The Shape of Portuguese 'Ultracolonialism'

Portugal's role in Africa is a study in contradiction. A small and underdeveloped European country, Portugal maintains possession of African territories which dwarf it in size and natural resources, some ten years after the wave of independence that swept over British, French, and Belgian colonies. Portugal was the first of the colonial powers to reach Africa, over four hundred years ago. But its control over Angola and Mozambique was only solidified in the early twentieth century, after others had initiated the 'scramble for Africa'. Portuguese propaganda proclaims a policy of non-racialism, and even exalts miscegenation. But the oppression suffered by Africans in Portuguese Africa is comparable to that under South Africa's rigid and explicitly racist *apartheid*. The uniqueness of Portuguese capacities for colonization is trumpeted to the world. But the economies of the 'overseas provinces', and even of Portugal itself, depend heavily on foreign capital and enterprise. Perry Anderson sums up Portugal's rule with the term 'ultracolonialism': 'at once the most *primitive* and the most *extreme* form of colonialism'.

The roots of this unique system go back to that 'marvellous century' when Portuguese navigators ventured farther and farther down the coast of Africa until finally, in 1498, Vasco da Gama rounded the Cape of Good Hope and crossed the Indian Ocean to India. And it was also a Portuguese captain, Fernão de Magalhães, who, a few years later, reached Asia from the other direction, around America. Such a beginning excited vast expectations, and on it a mythology was soon built. The epic poem by Camões, *Os Lusíadas*, celebrated the deeds of the heroes who discovered and conquered for Portugal an empire in the east.

Little known outside Portugal (except among scholars of literature), *Os Lusíadas* is in Portugal *the* classic. Schoolteachers in their classes compare it to Homer's *Odyssey* and Virgil's *Aeneid*. And its theme is empire.

That first empire consisted of little more than a string of fortified trading posts on the African and Asian coasts. From there Portuguese naval power dominated the trade of the Indian Ocean. The focus was the rich spice trade from the East; West Africa and Brazil (discovered in 1500) were as yet of only peripheral interest. The centre of the empire was Goa, on the western coast of India.

Goa remained Portuguese until 1961, when India recovered it by force. But even from the beginning, Portugal did not have the population or the resources to expand its control or maintain it against strong opposition. During the sixteenth century, there were probably never more than 10,000 Portuguese in the overseas empire. And although much money came to Lisbon, it did not stay there, to nourish the economy. It was the Dutch and the English who accumulated the capital that flowed through Lisbon. The Portuguese economy, says J. B. Trend in his history of Portugal, 'did not produce anything at home, in agriculture or manufacture; and in the midst of what seemed a perpetual carnival, the nation was begging its bread'. Even food had to be imported, and even the court was in debt.

The defeat and death of King Sebastião at the battle of Alcaçer Kebir in Morocco (1578) led to the assumption of the Portuguese Crown two years later by King Felipe II of Spain. For the next sixty years Portugal and Spain were under the same rulers. During the same time came the Dutch attack on Portugal's trade monopoly. Neither Portugal nor Spain could effectively compete with the economic resources and naval power available to their competitors. By mid-century the Dutch controlled a substantial part of the Asian trade; England and France were soon to follow. The focus of Portuguese empire shifted to Brazil, and to Angola, where the Dutch were repelled after a struggle in which Brazilians played a larger role than the Portuguese themselves. Angola and Brazil were tied together by the slave trade, which furnished the workers for the sugar plantations (and later for the mines) of Brazil. Angola was actually retaken from the Dutch by a Brazilian-led force in 1648, while Portugal was busy trying to defend its newly won independence from Spain.

Although Brazil's sugar, gold, and diamonds took the place of the lost income from the eastern trade, they still did not provide the basis for substantial development in Portugal. The 1703 Treaty of Methuen reveals Portugal's economic status; according to its terms Portuguese wines entered England at preferential rates, while in return Portugal gave free entry to English textiles. In a pattern more characteristic of a colony than of a colonial power, Portugal exported primary products, and imported manufactured goods. In spite of the income from Brazil, Portugal faced a chronic trade deficit. Much of its commerce was controlled by English merchants. And the necessity to import food continued.

At the beginning of the nineteenth century, the Napoleonic wars accentuated Portugal's decline. The Portuguese royal family fled to Brazil, which declared its independence several years later in 1822. Both Portugal and Brazil were then within the British 'sphere of influence'; but of the two, Brazil was more important and more prosperous. For Portugal the years that followed were ones of continued economic dependence, political instability, and recurrent financial crises or English interventions. The instability reached its peak in the chaotic republican era of 1910 to 1926, which saw forty-four governments come and go, as the urban elite played the game of politics. The mass of the Portuguese people remained uninvolved; and, with the advent of Salazar's *Estado Novo*, the problem of political transition to the modern world was solved by denying it. A stability based on repression was achieved: Salazar's dictatorial rule continued for forty years and the system he founded persists still, under his former associate Marcelo Caetano.

If, consistent with its general weakness, Portugal had retained into the twentieth century only isolated small imperial enclaves in Africa, as in Asia, it is unlikely that there would have been many problems in decolonization. Goa was easily taken by India when Portugal continued to ignore appeals to discuss the question. Macao in China, and Timor in Indonesia, are at the mercy of those countries, should they decide to take action. Even in Africa, the fort of São João Batista de Ajudá, on the coast of Dahomey, was easily taken from Portugal in 1961.

But during the 'scramble for Africa', Portugal not only retained the substantial enclave of 'Portuguese' Guinea, but also won control over the huge areas of Angola and Mozambique, extending inland from the traditional areas of Portuguese influence on the coast. England's occupation of Rhodesia and Nyasaland blocked Portuguese ambitions for a band of territory across Africa from east to west. But the command of Angola and Mozambique was ensured by the rivalry of other colonial powers among themselves. Even so, the precariousness of Portuguese control for some time is illustrated by a secret Anglo-German agreement (1898) to divide up Angola and Mozambique, if it should prove impossible to 'maintain their integrity'.

In the two decades preceding the First World War, Portuguese rule was consolidated in a series of battles against armed African resistance. The result is an empire in Africa consisting today of the islands of Cape Verde; 'Portuguese' Guinea on the mainland opposite the islands; São Tomé and Príncipe off the coast further south; Angola on the west coast; and Mozambique on the east. The most important are, of course, Angola and Mozambique, with a combined population

Table 1 *Populations and Areas of Portuguese Possessions*

	Population	*Area* (sq. miles)
Portugal	9,100,000	35,510
Angola	5,200,000	481,351
Mozambique	7,500,000	303,073
Guinea (Bissau)	544,000	14,000
Cape Verde	211,000	1,557
São Tomé and Príncipe	56,000	372

of 12 million and a combined area over twenty times that of Portugal.

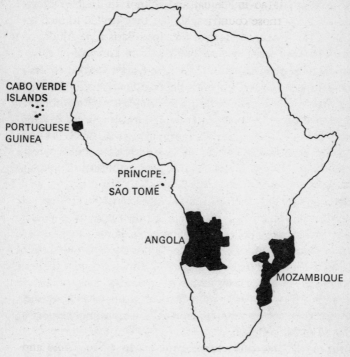

1. *Portugal's African Empire.*

Thus the contradiction: on the one hand Portugal has not yet entered the modern world, but remains economically dependent and politically rigid; on the other, it enlarged its empire in Africa at the same time as the more developed European powers, and maintains that empire still. The implications of Portugal's peculiar position can be seen in almost every aspect of its rule: in the hollowness of the claims of assimilation, in the notorious system of forced labour; and in the refusal ever to countenance the possibility of independence for the colonies. Portugal's 'primitive' lack of economic and political resources has led to the 'extreme' character of its colonial system. The oppression that results for the Africans under Portuguese rule cannot be concealed even by the overdeveloped mythology of the 'White Man's Burden, Portuguese-style'.

The Myth and Reality of Assimilation

Portugal's unique version of the White Man's Burden contrasts Portugal's lack of racialism with the position of the other European peoples. It aims at a future multiracial, multicontinental, and unified society – Portuguese in culture, language, and religion. 'The greatest source of Portuguese pride in Africa is a generally acknowledged lack of colour consciousness,' comments James Duffy in his highly respected book *Portuguese Africa*.

Such an ideology seems diametrically opposed to the racially separatist philosophy of the white supremacists who control South Africa and Rhodesia, neighbours to Portugal's Southern African colonies. But the response by the three to pressure for African rule is consistently negative. Military and economic cooperation is extensive, and still growing. The whites in Southern Africa join in a unified stand against black advance. The assertion of Portuguese non-racialism cannot, then, be accepted at face value.

The myth goes back particularly to the history of Brazil, where the openly accepted mixing of races contrasted sharply with the Anglo-Saxon horror of miscegenation expressed in North American society. Yet even in Brazil the remnants of slavery are visible in the general correspondence of class and colour lines. Lighter skin colour and higher status are still, by and large, associated. And in any case, Brazil, where a large mixed population has lived for centuries, cannot be convincingly compared with Portuguese Africa, where the Portuguese traded and raided for slaves, but only at the end of the nineteenth century conquered and began to settle.

The historical reality in Africa on which claims for a policy of non-racialism rest is much more meagre. The Portuguese in Africa before the twentieth century were few in number, and they seldom brought Portuguese women with them. Thus there was intermarriage of a kind. The *mistos* (mixed blood) and some few Africans became assimilated to Portuguese culture. Or, in some cases, Portuguese adventurers fitted themselves (as chiefs) into the African tribal structures. But these contacts did not mean the absence of discrimination or prejudice. Even Portuguese born in Asia, and the Asians themselves, did not always have the same rights in the religious orders, for example, as did the Portuguese from Europe. Africans have been, since the destruction of the Kingdom of the Kongo by Portuguese slavers, considered primarily as slaves, naturally inferior and fitted above all for manual labour.

One of the men who in the 1890s set the pattern for Portuguese colonial administration expressed his views like this:

It is true that the generous soul of Wilberforce [the English anti-slavery crusader] has not transmigrated into my body, but I don't believe I have in me the blood of a slaver: I even feel an inner fondness for the Negro, this big child, instinctively bad like all children ... though docile and sincere. I do not consider him something to be exterminated because of the necessity for the expansion of the white race, although I may believe in natural inferiority.

(ANTONIO ENES, *Moçambique*, p. 75)

And Marcelo Caetano, now Salazar's successor as Premier, visited Mozambique in his capacity as Minister of Colonies in 1945. He reminded the colonists that it was Portugal's policy to accept fully 'assimilated' Africans (apparently they were tending to forget the policy); but he also advised them that:

on one point only should we be rigorous with respect to racial separation: namely marital or casual sexual mixing of blacks and whites, the source of serious disturbances in social life, and of the serious problem of race mixing; serious, I say, if not from the biological point of view, so controversial and on which it's not for me to take a position, then at least from the sociological point of view.

(MARCELO CAETANO, *Alguns Discursos*, p. 57)

Portuguese racial prejudice is not as closely tied to the idea of race, as such, as is the racism of northern Europeans. Nor is its expression unambiguous. But it clearly exists. And the scorn for Africans inherent in the Portuguese attitudes can be seen in the very mechanism which is proposed for attaining the 'multi-racial' unity of the Portuguese nation. That mechanism is assimilation: not through the creation of some new culture, but through becoming Portuguese, absorbing Portuguese culture and language.

To become an *assimilado* involved, until shortly after the beginning of the war in Angola, a considerable procedure. An applicant had to prove his ability to speak and write correct Portuguese; show that he had a certain income; submit a number of documents and certificates; and finally pay a fee. Only then could the African become a Portuguese citizen. The Portuguese settler, who might be illiterate and unable to satisfy such qualifications himself, did not have to worry about such a test: he was already a Portuguese citizen.

Even the *assimilado* does not find himself in a position of full equality with white Portuguese. He has to carry an identity card with him to *prove* that he is a citizen. Whites carry their proof in the colour of their skin. He is often paid less, even when doing the same job as a white. He must learn to reject his own background, and listen quietly or join in Portuguese remarks about 'primitive' natives. Eduardo Mondlane, the late President of the Mozambique Liberation Front, commented that 'the most that the *assimilado* system even sets out to do is to create a few "honorary whites", and this certainly does not constitute non-racialism' (*The Struggle for Mozambique*, p. 50).

The statistics show on how slight a base is built the claim of a population becoming Portuguese by intermarriage and assimilation. The percentage of mixed origin is greater in South Africa (the 'Coloureds' make up 8 per cent of the population) than in Angola and Mozambique. The absolute numbers are not large either: in 1960 there were 50,000 *mistos* in Angola, and 30,000 in Mozambique. One cannot build a Brazil on that.

The number of assimilated Africans is even smaller. In Angola the 1950 census recorded some 30,000 *assimilado*; while Mozambique had less than 5,000 (the status of *assimilados* is not included in the 1960 census reports). A Portuguese study of Mozambique divided the population there as follows:

1. a minority of about 2.5%, consisting of whites, Asians, mulattoes and a few Africans concentrated in the urban areas;
2. a larger group of some 3.5%, forming the urban and plantation working class, almost all African; and
3. the 94% of the population, entirely African, engaged primarily in subsistence agriculture, supplemented by some form of migrant labour and some cash crops.

(PROMOÇÃO SOCIAL EM MOÇAMBIQUE, quoted in *The Struggle for Mozambique*, p. 38)

In Angola the percentage in the second category is likely to be larger, owing to the greater development of a mining and cash crop economy. But the structure of the pyramid, and the basic distribution of privilege among its diverse levels, is much the same.

The vast majority of Africans who do not qualify for assimilation live under special regulations for the *indigenas* (natives). In 1961, this special system was abolished, at least on paper, and all Africans were made Portuguese citizens. However, those who were citizens before 1961 and those who were not, received different types of identity cards, so that the police can still easily distinguish one category from the other. By means of this passbook, movement of Africans from one district to another, or from the rural areas to the urban centres, is rigidly controlled. The control might not be quite as efficient as the similar passbook system in South Africa, but its intent is the same – the control of a large population of Africans by a white regime. The 'native' African is also subject to punishment at the discretion of the local Portuguese administrator, and, perhaps most important of all, to the system of forced labour.

Forced Labour: A Modern Slavery

Neither slavery and the slave trade, nor the later practice of forced labour, are uniquely Portuguese. Portugal has perhaps rightly resented the hypocrisy of other European powers in criticizing her for what they were doing only a few years before. But it is still true that these institutions take on a prominence in Portuguese colonial history only occasionally attained by other countries.

Angola's history in particular has been scarred by the slave trade. The early promising relationships of the Portuguese with the King of the Kongo soon collapsed as the market for slaves became more profitable than any other relationship. Priests, soldiers, and traders vied with one another to make a profit. It is estimated that from 1580 to 1836 over four million Africans were exported from the region of the Congo and Angola, and over three million from Angola alone. The slave was the basic item of commerce, and the cause of wars in the interior. In most of West Africa it was rare for the European trader to venture far from the coast; he obtained enough slaves from his bargaining at the coastal markets. But Portugal did not have the quantity or quality of goods to offer that the English or the Dutch did. Partly for this reason, perhaps, in Angola wars were stirred up by traders or by the colonial administration as substantial alternate sources of supply. On the Nigerian coast, some African states grew rich on the trade, while others were devastated; in Angola, devastation was general.

In Angola, too, the transition from slavery meant at first little more than a change of name. In 1903, Henry Nevinson, travelling in Angola, still found slaves being exported to São Tomé for work on the cocoa plantations, more than thirty years after the official abolition of slavery. The Africans who were sent to São Tomé were legally *serviçães* (indentured servants), who had signed a contract for five years. But Nevinson quotes one conversation on shipboard:

> 'Why are you here?'
>   'We were sold to the white men.'
> 'Did you come of your own free will?'
>   'Of course not.'
> 'Where did you come from?'
>   'From Bihé.'

'Are you slaves or not?'
'Of course we are slaves!'

(HENRY NEVINSON, *A Modern Slavery*, p. 184)

Protest by English humanitarians, and even a boycott of São Tomé cocoa led by the Quaker chocolate manufacturer Cadbury, brought an end to this trade before 1917, although the shortage of labour for use in Angola itself may also have been a contributing factor. But the practice of forced labour continued in Angola. It was rationalized as a way of making the lazy African civilize himself by work. The Labour Regulation of 1899 put it like this:

All natives of Portuguese overseas provinces are subject to the moral and legal obligation of attempting to obtain through work the means that they lack to subsist and to better their social condition. They have full liberty to choose the method of fulfilling this obligation, but if they do not fulfil it, public authority may force a fulfilment.

In other words, unemployment (which included in practice subsistence farming) became a crime.

Similar practices were not unknown in other colonial territories – the horrors of rubber production in King Leopold's Congo were equal to anything in Portuguese Africa – but France and England, and finally Belgium, succeeded in creating a cash economy that made 'forced labour' steadily less important. Not so, however, even now, in Portuguese Africa. Visitors to Angola in the 1950s (Basil Davidson, Gwendolyn Carter, John Gunther) reported the forced recruitment of African workers for the colonial administration and for the white-owned plantations. Henrique Galvão, a Portuguese administrator in Angola, had in 1947 presented a report attacking forced labour practices. Marvin Harris, in 1958 and again in 1967, documented the continuation of forced labour practices in Mozambique, in spite of paper reforms.

Angola's forced labour system has attracted more attention. But it is Mozambique which most clearly shows the variety of ways in which the system is used to exploit African labour. The disguises have changed over the years. In theory, 'forced labour' has been illegal since 1897. In reality it continues unabated. Based on the assumption that the African must not remain idle, and on the lack of any effective curb to the power of the local officials who administer the system, it raises multitudes of African workers: for the mines in South Africa, for the roads and plantations of Mozambique itself, and for the cultivation of cotton destined for the Portuguese textile industry. The African subsistence farmer is presumed to be 'idle'. Only the possession of sufficient cattle, or the cultivation of a significant quantity of a cash crop, provides exemption from the necessity to take another job. Few Africans can meet these qualifications; most are engaged simply in raising food for themselves and their families.

One way to fulfil the obligation to work, open to those in southern Mozambique, is to be recruited by the Witwatersrand Native Labour Association (WNLA), for work in the mines of South Africa. Mozambican Africans account for about one-third of the labour force in mining there. Even the low wages paid to African miners in South Africa are much better than most Africans receive in Mozambique; and there are usually workers slipping across the border as well as those passing through the official recruitment channels. On the official level, the South African government guarantees that 47.5 per cent of the sea-borne import traffic to the Johannesburg area will pass through Lourenço Marques, in return for the privilege of recruiting an average of 100,000 workers per year. Portugal also receives a bonus payment for each recruit, with half of his wages, to be paid him on his return to Mozambique.

The result of this labour migration to South Africa, and (on a lesser scale) to Rhodesia, is that 'something like two-thirds of the mature, able-bodied men of Southern Mozambique are employed in foreign territories' (Marvin Harris, *Portugal's African Wards*, p. 29). As the men do not earn enough to buy food for their families at home, and cannot take their families with them to the mines, the food must be grown by those who stay at home. It is a very 'efficient' arrangement. Otherwise the South African mine-owners might have to pay subsistence for families and not just single men, and it might not be so profitable to extract the gold for the world's money markets.

If the African worker does not go to South Africa, he may end up working on a sugar or a tea plantation. Joaquim Maquival tells how it was for his family:

> We had to work on the government land; at least it isn't government land, it belongs to a company, but it was the government which made us work on it. It was the land of the Sociedade de Chá Oriental de Milange. The government came and arrested us in our villages and sent us to the company; that is, the company paid money to the administration or the government, and then the government arrested us and gave us to the company. I began working for the company when I was twelve; they paid me fifteen escudos a month (53¢). I worked from six in the morning until twelve noon, when we stopped for two hours; then again from two p.m. until six p.m. The whole family worked for the company; my brothers, my father – my father is still there. My father earned and still earns 150 escudos a month ($5.30). He had to pay 195 escudos tax yearly. We didn't want to work for the company, but if we refused the government sent the police to the villages, and they arrested those who refused, and if they ran away the government circulated photographs and a hunt was started. When they caught them they beat them and put them in prison, and when they came out of prison they had to go and work but without pay; they said that as they ran away they didn't need the money. Thus in our own fields only our mothers were left, who could not do much. ... We had neither sugar nor tea – we had to work on the tea but we didn't know what it tasted like. Tea never came to our houses. (Quoted in *The Struggle for Mozambique*, p. 87)

Joaquim's father worked under what is called 'contract labour', in which the labourer is recruited under contract supervised by the administration. Failure to fulfil one's obligations under the contract, or other offences, may lead to conviction in court, and to a sentence of unpaid 'correctional labour', another category of work. There is also 'obligatory labour', officially abolished since 1961, but still used to get workers for roads and other public works. The residual category of employment, a direct relationship with an employer such as in domestic service, is called 'voluntary labour'.

Labour export to neighbouring countries, and the use of African workers on plantations, were less important in the north of Mozambique than in the south and centre. In the north forced cultivation of cotton took over as the dominant mode of labour exploitation. Gabriel Nantimbo tells how the system operated in his experience:

I was born in Imbuho, a cotton-growing region, in 1942. . . . My whole family produced cotton for the Companhia Agrícola Algodoeira. When the company came to exploit our region everyone was forced to cultivate one field of cotton. Each person was given seeds. Then one had to clear the field, thin the cotton, and then remove the weeds. Finally, after the harvest the company told us where to take the cotton and then bought it from us. They paid us very little for it. It was extremely difficult to make a living because we were badly paid and we didn't have the time to look after other crops: cotton needs constant attention; you have to keep weeding the field and thinning out the plants. . . .

We were forced to produce cotton. The people didn't want to: they knew that cotton is the mother of poverty but the company was protected by the government. We knew that anyone who refused to grow it would be sent to the plantations of São Tomé where he would work without any pay at all. So as not to make our poverty even greater, then, so as not to leave the family and leave the children to suffer alone, we had to grow cotton. My uncle had a field of cotton like everyone else. One day he fell sick and could not look after the field. The company manager sent him to the authorities and he told them he was sick. The administrator said to him, 'you're a bad man. What you want is to avoid work. Do you think others don't fall sick? Is everyone who works the fields in good health?' My uncle replied, 'There are different sorts of illness. With some you can go on working, with others you can't. I couldn't work.' They arrested my uncle and sent him to São Tomé for a year. (Quoted in *Mozambique Revolution*, February–March 1968)

The pay is low, as low as $3 for the entire harvest, according to the former Bishop of Beira. And famine has sometimes resulted from the concentration on cotton to the neglect of food crops. But then Portugal's textile mills receive their supplies at less than world market prices.

In Angola and Mozambique the Portuguese, still unable to provide adequate incentives to get Africans to work for them, continue to use coercion to make up the labour force. As in the days of slavery, or when *serviçães* made their involuntary trips to São Tomé, the African is still, above all else, the *'mão d'obra'* (workhand). Economic developments have decreased the use of overt forms of forced labour, as more Africans are incorporated into the money economy. But neither the mythology of assimilation nor recurrent paper reforms have changed substantially this basic reality; nor can they succeed in hiding it.

Assimilation Strategies?

It would be unfair to say that the Portuguese are making no attempt at all to put their scheme of assimilation into effect. But it is clear that the measures taken to do so are inappropriate, and handicapped by Portugal's lack of financial and human resources. Neither settlers nor schools are likely to bring about the dream of African 'provinces' becoming fully Portuguese.

One way to make Africa more Portuguese is, it is assumed, to bring more Portuguese from Europe. Thus Portuguese plans for the development of the Zambezi River valley call for one million Portuguese settlers after the completion of the Cabora Bassa hydroelectric project. One study even suggested that such settlement would help stop the 'denationalizing' influence of Islam, confining it to north of the river. White population has already grown significantly during the years from 1930 to 1960: in Angola from 30,000 to almost 200,000; in Mozambique from 18,000 to approximately 85,000. Now soldiers who have finished their terms of service are encouraged to stay and settle on readily available land. Although Portuguese emigrants still prefer Brazil, or France, increasing numbers are coming to Africa.

But the principal result is not going to be assimilation. The number of immigrants remains small compared with total population of Angola or Mozambique. But it is large enough for the Portuguese minority frequently to fill not only the higher administrative and economic positions, but also skilled and even unskilled ones. Many of the immigrants are illiterate; and what skill they may have, as in farming, is unsuited for tropical conditions. Such men are therefore, at least for some time, on the same level as Africans, and in competition with them. This competition, combined with the greater privileges generally accorded to the immigrant, heightens racial tension.

The stereotypes that develop are clear from Marvin Harris's observation that 'the clear majority of whites in Moçambique regard the Negro as inferior and accept his inferior social position as irrefutable proof of the fact.' The indiscriminate reprisals taken against Africans by white vigilante groups in Angola in 1961 reveal the same kind of sentiment. If Portuguese non-racialism ever really existed, a greater influx of white settlers is more likely to destroy than to promote it. Placing settlers in competition with Africans cannot help but increase racial hostilities. The Portuguese might have learnt at least that from the experience of other colonial powers.

Settlement seems unlikely, on the face of it, to encourage assimilation. With education, the position is more ambiguous. Education, if available to substantial numbers of Africans and rewarded by suitable employment after its completion, might produce a group of Africans committed to some form of co-operation with the Portuguese. Certainly the French experience in Vietnam, and in Africa, points to such a possibility. If Portugal were to grant such independence as that received by most of the former French colonies in tropical Africa, it might even be possible to increase the number of whites, and maintain Portuguese influence. There are for instance far more French expatriates in the Ivory Coast now, than under imperial rule. It is some such solution, indeed, which Portugal's western allies might like to see adopted. But they are likely to be disappointed.

For even elementary education is still confined to a minority of the African population: and at secondary and university level, education is overwhelmingly white. This remains true despite the expansion of education after the shock of the first outbreak in Angola. Illiteracy rates in the 1950s were over 95 per cent. Portugal claims that these have been substantially reduced since then, but there are no reliable figures. And two or three years in a primary school makes for dubious literacy, especially when classes are taught in a foreign language. The majority of Africans who do enter the four-year primary course drop out before the final year.

Statistics giving a racial breakdown of school enrolment are not available for Angola; and for Mozambique the latest year published is 1964–5. But these are revealing enough. In Mozambique, out of 7,827 students in academic secondary schools (5th to 11th grades) in 1964–5, only 636 (8 per cent) were Africans. Of the 321 students in the university-level *Estudos Gerais Universitários*, exactly 4 (about 1 per cent) were African. Although detailed statistics for more recent years are not yet available, the total growth of education at all upper levels is still so small that even if the entire increase in enrolment were African, the percentage of Africans could hardly approach their percentage of the total population. An article in the *New York Times* of 9 August 1969 reported a 15 per cent African element in the university. And the racial ratio in Angola is reputed to be largely similar to that in Mozambique.

Primary schools are expanding more rapidly, and do contain, by necessity, a majority of Africans. The distinction between 'official' schools and the schools run by the Catholic missions for Africans still means, however, that most Africans get a second-class education. The curricula and official examinations may be the same; but the facilities available are not. The pattern of primary school enrolment for 1966/7 is shown by these figures from Angola:

Total: 264,836 pupils, of whom
First year: 173,124
Second year: 45,193
Third year: 27,969
Fourth year: 18,550
(Passing fourth-year exams: 4,279)

Moreover, the curricula and teaching methods are little adapted to African conditions. The principal aim of primary education is still 'to teach the Portuguese language, to inculcate Portuguese values and to develop in the pupils a conscious identification with Portugal in order to strengthen national unity'. And secondary-school textbooks used are still the same as those used in Portugal. At all levels the African child is likely to learn more about the history, geography, and even the flora and fauna of metropolitan Portugal than of his own country (or province, as the Portuguese would say). Even in terms of the Portuguese theory of one multicontinental and multi-racial state, school-children in Mozambique should, surely, learn more about the Zambezi River in their own land than about the Tagus River in far-away European Portugal. They do not.

Thus the expansion of education is both too small and too late to provide large numbers of genuine converts to Portuguese 'civilization'. A war of liberation has already started in each of the Portuguese African colonies, and most of Africa has already gained its political independence. It is too late for many people to acquiesce in a total denial of their own cultural heritage. One can reasonably expect such a result neither from the larger numbers who go to primary school nor from the few Africans who attend secondary schools designed primarily for their white contemporaries.

As strategies for assimilation, increasing white settlement and increasing education may buy some time for the Portuguese in their counter-insurgency effort. But they will not make African peoples Portuguese.

Portuguese Intransigence: Is There a Reason?

In the years following the Second World War, American talk of anti-colonialism, when it was not emphasizing the dangers of 'premature independence', touched again and again on the theme of mutually profitable relationships between mother country and politically independent ex-colonies. As Britain in the nineteenth century maintained its influence through an 'Empire of Free Trade', the United States saw similar possibilities for the twentieth century. The Monroe Doctrine in Latin America and the Open Door in the Far East were already examples of such influence without formal control. The United States advised its European allies that they, too, should perhaps move to such a model, and eliminate the tempting target that 'colonialism' made for the spread of communism and revolution.

Recognizing the changed realities of the postwar world, most of the colonial powers moved, eventually, in this direction. They succeeded in retaining, for the most part, substantial influence in their ex-colonies. But Portugal has not taken this step. Economic backwardness and political rigidity have been basic in determining this stance of Portuguese colonialism.

Economic backwardness does not mean that the Portuguese ruling sectors derive no profit from Africa. It means rather that if independence were granted, the advantages presently enjoyed could not be preserved for Portugal by the more sophisticated methods of economic and political influence used by the other powers. Such benefits include the contribution made by Africa to the Portuguese balance of payments; the terms of trade between Portugal and the 'overseas provinces'; and the high profit obtained from diamonds, oil, iron, and other minerals yet to be discovered.

Metropolitan Portugal's balance of trade with foreign countries is consistently in deficit. And this deficit is partially made up for metropolitan Portugal by a strong surplus balance of trade with the 'overseas provinces'. Without the 'overseas provinces', Portugal would face continuing difficulties in this area.

The income earned for Portugal by Angola and Mozambique comes mainly from export of primary commodities and African labour; secondarily, from their role in transport for South Africa, Rhodesia, Zambia, and the Congo. Angola exports coffee, diamonds, iron ore, and oil to world markets. Mozambique's most important exports are all agricultural: cashew nuts, sugar, tea, sisal. Labour export to South Africa is important for the income of Mozambique, especially since part of the payment is in gold. The role of Mozambique's ports (Lourenço Marques and Beira) as outlets for South Africa and Rhodesia is very significant; Angola's Benguela Railway plays a similar role for the mining areas of Zambia and Katanga.

Portugal profits not only from the income gained by Angola and Mozambique, but also from the pattern of trade established with them. The Portuguese textile industry gets its cotton from Angola and Mozambique, then sells back to them the finished products. The conditions under which that cotton is produced, and the prices paid to the African producers, have already been discussed (see page 26 ff.). Other trade items with which Portugal is supplied include sugar and oilseeds. Portuguese wine, tinned fish, chemicals, and rubber products find a protected market in the colonies.

Perhaps of even more eventual significance are the mineral resources now being opened up. The diamonds of Angola are a traditional export; but iron and petroleum are new, and the production of these is growing rapidly. As exploration for new resources continues, further discoveries can be expected. The income for the Portuguese state, and for those Portuguese companies and individuals involved, represents an important new stake in Africa.

But these advantages for particular Portuguese interests depend on cooperation with particular interests from other Western countries. Even in the initial stages of Portuguese colonization, major enterprises were under foreign control. In Angola, the Benguela Railway and the Angola Diamond Company are under the control of British, South African, and Belgian financial interests. In 1966 the Angola Diamond Company alone provided approximately 5 per cent of government revenue in Angola. In Mozambique, Sena Sugar Estates, the largest producer of sugar in the country, is British-owned. Earlier in the century the Mozambique and Niassa Companies, with British, French, and German capital, had responsibility for economic development and even government control over much of the country.

Indeed, in Portugal itself there is substantial foreign command of the economy. The largest producer of wolfram is a former British company, recently acquired by the Anglo-American Corporation of South Africa. The main producer of tyres is controlled by General Tire and Rubber of Ohio. The public transport system of Lisbon is run by a British company. S A C O R, which runs the principal petroleum refinery in Portugal, is two-thirds controlled by French interests.

More recently, the spurt of development in Angola and Mozambique is based almost entirely on foreign investment. The searchers for oil are American, French, German, South African; those who exploit and refine it are American, French, Belgian. The increased production of iron has been conducted by international investment, with Fried. Krupp of West Germany at the head. The hydroelectric and irrigation projects on the Cunene and Zambezi Rivers are dependent on South African direction, and finance from South Africa and Europe. From Portugal itself, reports the Organization for Economic Cooperation and Development, 'the real net flow of private capital to the overseas provinces is not very appreciable' (*OECD Economic Survey: Portugal*, 1966).

This pattern of foreign involvement means that the 'neo-colonial' option is effectively eliminated for Portugal. The United States has long recommended to more traditional colonial powers that informal means of influence, 'mutually advantageous relationships' such as the United States enjoys with Latin America, are much better suited to the modern world than direct colonial control. But such influence depends on economic power: the ability to provide 'aid'; to control enterprises through technicians as well as investment; to maintain good trade relationships by pressure on susceptible governments; to support with open or covert action the removal of governments that prove troublesome.

France, Britain, Belgium, and the Netherlands have applied such a strategy with varying degrees of success. France's relationship with many of her former colonies illustrates best the ability to maintain influence and even exclude the other capitalist powers. But Portugal would stand very little chance of applying such a strategy with success. The foreign interests involved would, if Angola and Mozambique were independent, have little incentive to channel their dealings through Lisbon. They would still promote 'cooperative' governments, and do what they could to prevent revolutionary economic policies from being implemented. But even that would not operate to the benefit of *Portuguese* interests, which could hardly compete with South African, American, and Western European capital.

Thus Portugal's economic backwardness is an important factor in sustaining the Portuguese refusal to grant independence. But it is not a sufficient explanation. For not all of Portugal benefits, of course, from the maintenance of colonialism. Among the mass of Portuguese there is little eagerness to emigrate to Africa; even less, to risk death there in a colonial war. Nor is the more than 50 per cent of the national budget devoted to war helping the Portuguese people, as it might if devoted to education and development in Portugal itself. Even some sectors of the Portuguese business leadership would rather cast in their lot with the European Common Market than fight to the bitter end in Africa.

But in the Portuguese political system, there is small opportunity for expression of such dissent. The professional military, which established the Salazarist dictatorship over forty years ago, have become even more important with their expansion to fight the wars in Africa. Such wars are their main task, and indeed their *raison d'être*. They consider the idea of abandoning Portuguese 'glory' and 'honour' in Africa only as treason. And the police state system continues to function after Salazar's death, despite all Caetano's supposed liberalization as depicted by the Western press.

In the Assembly elections of 1969, the official National Union party won all 130 seats. Registered voters included 1.8 million in Portugal itself (from a population of 9 million); while in the 'overseas provinces' of Angola, Mozambique, and Guinea, the number of registered voters ranged from one to three per cent of the population. Although there were some opposition candidates, political parties were still forbidden; and restrictions placed on campaigning severely hampered opposition activities. (For example, no discussion of the war or colonial policy was permitted.) Some forty per cent of the registered voters abstained.

Such a political system is accompanied by the usual apparatus of a police state: censorship of press and books, a security police (the infamous P I D E, now called the General Office of Security), trained in the 1930s by the Gestapo; prisons and prison camps in Portugal and overseas. Prisoners are often taken to prisons in another part of the 'Portuguese space'. An Angolan in Timor, or a Mozambican in Lisbon, or a Portuguese in Cape Verde, is effectively cut off from contact with his family and friends. Nor is there an 'excessive' concern with legality; individuals may disappear without trial, or the knowledge of their families, if they are suspected of subversive activities.

Protest is thus forced underground. In Africa it has taken the form of armed struggle. In Portugal, resistance often means exile, an escape to France or Algeria. Military service is practically universal for young men, and for a large number of older men as well (the upper age limit for the draft is forty-five). Resistance, though unpublicized, is substantial. Deserters and draft-dodgers reached some 15,000 in 1967; and the numbers continue to increase.

The lack of opportunity for open protest is matched, among those committed to the *status quo*, by an extreme rigidity of thought, based on the idea that political independence for Africans would be an unthinkable treason, a betrayal of the Portuguese mission in the world. Dr Sid Gilchrist, a Canadian doctor and missionary in Angola for most of his life, outlines two basic assumptions in the outlook:

We became aware of a universal pattern of delusion in the European mind that seemed to us a kind of mass psychopathic phenomenon. . . . Certain basic assumptions and convictions seem ingrained in almost all Portuguese colonists, professional people and administrators, newly arrived or African-born, lofty or lowly. One of these is that the African is mentally and morally inferior to the Portuguese. . . . Another seemingly universal false assumption that one meets everywhere among the Portuguese, and especially among the better educated, is that they, the Portuguese, in their dealings with the Africans are superior to all other colonizing peoples. They whole-heartedly believe that they have a unique natural gift for under-standing the African, for establishing rapport with him, and for making him an adoring, obedient and grateful ward.

(*Angola Awake*, p. 60)

The Portuguese might reply that this is the typical prejudice of a Protestant missionary. But the fact remains, attested by the African struggle itself, that Portugal is living under a delusion. Those who suffer from the consequences of the delusion can hardly be expected to wait patiently for their masters to recover their sanity by some internal process.

2 American Policy Under Truman and Eisenhower: The Irrelevance of Self-determination

'The right of each nation to govern itself has been the most traditional of all principles in American thinking.... American sympathies have always been strongly in favour of colonial peoples aspiring to independence' (William Reitzel, *United States Foreign Policy*, p. 27). So goes a not untypical statement of American foreign policy. The Atlantic Charter, agreed to by Roosevelt and Churchill on 14 August 1941, puts it like this:

They [the signatories] respect the right of all peoples to choose the form of government under which they will live; and they wish to see sovereign rights and self-government restored to those who have been forcibly deprived of them.

Churchill, and others among the subsequent signatories (twenty-six countries), may have thought it referred only to Europe. President Roosevelt, however, declared that it was meant to apply universally.

With a remarkable consistency, whether one considers the issue of democratic self-determination in Portugal itself, or the subject of independence for its colonies, such principles proved irrelevant to the development of US–Portuguese relations.

The Second World War, Portugal, and George Kennan

Under Salazar, Portugal's ties with the Axis powers were carefully ambiguous. During the Spanish Civil War, the Salazar regime gave strong support to the Franco forces, facilitating the flow of military supplies to them. The secret police benefited from Gestapo training. There was wide sympathy for the fanatic anti-communism of the Nazi and Fascist forces; and although the ruling ideology in Portugal was not identical with that in Germany and Italy, there were strong family resemblances. Salazar felt strongly that the West was wrong in opposing Germany on ideological (that is, democratic) grounds, instead of recognizing the real common enemy – the Soviet Union. As late as 1949, when proposing the acceptance of NATO to the Portuguese National Assembly, he referred to the wartime decision of the Allies to crush Germany as a 'dangerous policy'.

Yet Portugal's closest ties were still with Britain, and throughout the war Salazar followed an explicitly neutralist line. American and British policy was directed first of all at inducing Portugal to maintain that neutrality, and then to go beyond strict neutrality by stopping the export of wolfram to Germany. Wolfram is a major source of tungsten, crucial for modern steel production, and was therefore of strategic importance to both the Allies and the Axis. At first the issue was settled by allocating the export of mines controlled by British capital to the Allies, and the export of mines controlled by German capital to Germany. Later, in 1944, Portugal, seeing the trend of the conflict, and succumbing to pressure from Britain, the United States, and Brazil, agreed to embargo wolfram exports to Germany.

The priority of military-strategic interests carried over to a subject of even more interest to the Allies: the Azores. These North Atlantic islands, it was calculated, must not be allowed to fall into German hands, lest trans-Atlantic sea routes be disrupted. Rumours of American contingency plans to occupy the Azores (should Spain join Hitler, and Portugal come under German control) reached Portugal early in the war, and aroused strong reactions. Later, the islands became important also to Allied plans for the Normandy invasion, and as a stop-over point for planes on the way to the Far East. Britain, in 1943, invoked the ancient alliance with Portugal, and began negotiations for an airbase.

In August 1943, the British negotiations were brought to a successful conclusion; in October British troops landed in the Azores to prepare Lagens Field, on Terceira Island, for use by military aircraft. The United States then began its negotiations for similar facilities. In mid-1943 the American minister to Lisbon, Mr Bert Fish, had died, and chargé d'affaires George Kennan became responsible for the negotiations. His attitudes, as recorded in his *Memoirs: 1925–1950*, are of importance not only because they reveal the assumptions of policy-makers at that time, but because of his subsequent importance as one of the chief theoreticians in the Cold War.*

The story, as told by Kennan, is a case study in failure of communication within the US diplomatic service. He was first told to assure the integrity of the Portuguese empire; then told not to; did anyway; was called to Washington (but not for that reason); and finally straightened matters out through a talk with President Roosevelt, who wrote a personal letter to Salazar declaring that the United States would of course leave the Azores again once the war was over. What is perhaps most interesting is that the option of *not* respecting Portuguese sovereignty brought to Kennan's mind only the possibility that the United States might take the Azores by force. The question of progress towards independence for Portugal's African or Asian colonies evidently did not occur to him. The assurance given by Kennan stated, however, that 'the United States of America undertakes to respect Portuguese sovereignty in *all*† Portuguese colonies' (*Department of State Bulletin*, 1946, p. 1082).

Equally revealing of the assumptions that would shape post-war relations with Portugal are the attitudes that Kennan reveals in his memoirs towards the Salazarist regime itself. He refers to Salazar respectfully as a man of principle, and is eager to explain away the fact that some stories in the American press had labelled him a fascist. His long-term concern was to see the Anglo-Portuguese Alliance extended to close relationships with the United States, given the common security interests in the Atlantic. One can find in Kennan's account no indication at all that he was in the least concerned with either Portugal's domestic

---

*In the January 1971 issue of *Foreign Affairs*, Kennan, consistent with his past attitudes, came out against even the token support given by the United States to the African cause in southern Africa, saying that it might lead to violence.

†My italics.

dictatorship or any future self-determination for Portugal's colonies.

Such determination of policy by military and security interests alone may perhaps be disillusioning to idealists fresh from the reading of the Atlantic Charter, or still steeped in similar passages from their high-school history text books. But it is hardly surprising in view of the general trends of American policy. The applicability of such ideals has been severely selective: confined to where political forces have compelled them to be taken into account, or where they could be profitably employed against an opponent. Thus self-determination was much talked of when it was a question of keeping Greece and Turkey out of the Soviet sphere of influence. And even the Dutch found themselves confronted with American anti-colonialism when it seemed that 'Indonesia and Southeast Asia generally could be saved from communism only if the colonial powers were strongly pressed to follow a policy of withdrawal' (William Reitzel, *United States Foreign Policy*, p. 226). Even Portugal might have heard of self-determination from the United States, had the other side won in the Spanish Civil War, and, together with the Soviet Union, backed a guerrilla movement that threatened to oust Salazar.

But Portugal and its colonies remained untouched by such currents. They were doubly peripheral. The Portuguese possessions in Asia were small, and of little interest as long as larger areas were still under colonial rule. Africa as a whole was not very significant to American strategic concerns; and in any case the nationalist unrest that was emerging in other colonies seemed to have little echo in the Portuguese territories. Portugal itself was neither an important European power, nor situated on the edge of the Soviet sphere of influence. Its only claim to American attention was the Azores.

Independence for Africa ?

Independence for Africa was, for long, of little concern to American policy-makers. There was a report, written for the Phelps-Stokes Fund by a committee of churchmen and educators, on the Atlantic Charter and Africa. Its eight points, presented in 1942, included the goal of ultimate self-government; the importance of immediate steps in that direction; and the establishment, in the US Department of State, of an African Bureau to deal with such questions. The Africa Bureau was not established until 1958, however; and, in general, more weight seems to have been given to the perspective of another report. Prepared for the Council on Foreign Relations in 1944, it stated 'the case for leaving the task of leadership in this field to those countries which have most at stake therein' (*The American Interest in the 'Colonial Problem'*, p. 12).

The countries so referred to were, of course, not the African countries themselves, but the European colonial powers. The primary interest was in Europe, and it was considered important not to antagonize the major allies of the United States. Hans Morgenthau, in a 1955 critique of US Africa policy, observed that 'the United States had tended to opt in virtually all respects for the policies of the metropolitan powers ... and it has subordinated its long-range interest in the autonomous development of the native population to short-range considerations of strategy and expediency' (in *Africa in the Modern World*, p. 321). As late as 1961 William Attwood, newly appointed Ambassador to Guinea, was informed by his fellow diplomats that 'our policy... was still to tailor our actions in Africa to the wishes of our often short-sighted NATO partners' (*The Reds and the Blacks*, p. 16).

As shown by Morgenthau and Attwood, even the critique of such policy rested on accusations of 'short-sightedness'. As Assistant Secretary of State Bryoade put it in 1953,

Since old-style colonialism is on its way out, and nothing can restore it, the real choice today lies between continued progress towards self-determination and surrender to the Communist imperialism.

(*Department of State Bulletin*, 1953, p. 656)

'Premature independence', however, was even worse than colonial short-sightedness, for it might open a road to communism. Any independence that came in opposition to the colonial powers, and prevented the emergence of 'mutually beneficial' relations between mother country and ex-colony, was *a priori* premature.

Even this largely negative position on self-determination referred essentially to non-Portuguese colonies. The peripheral character of Portugal was well illustrated in the previously mentioned report from the Council on Foreign Relations, which emphasized that 'it will be important for us not to antagonize France, Holland, Belgium, etc.' (*The American Interest in the 'Colonial Problem'*, p. 12). Britain had been mentioned earlier; but Portugal, it seems, fitted in only as part of the 'etc.'. American policy-makers had to give at least an occasional thought to self-determination in other colonies. But the un-importance of Portugal, and the absence in the Portuguese colonies of any nationalist sentiment visible to the outside world, meant that self-determination there was not even presented to U S policy-makers as an issue to consider.

Portugal's Inclusion in NATO

Portugal was not an important ally for the United States. But it did soon become a close friend, and escaped even the con-sequences which Italy, as a defeated power, or Spain, as an ostracized dictatorship, faced. Italy lost Libya; and, because the Soviet Union offered itself as a candidate for trusteeship power, the West even supported an early independence for the territory instead. In terms of the criteria for independence so often mentioned (education, administrative preparation, etc.), Libya was certainly less prepared than many other African states. By the tacit criterion of readiness to maintain economic and military ties with the West, however, it was not likely to be accused of 'premature independence'.

Spain was another question. Spain and Portugal both main-tained dictatorial regimes and openly condemned democracy. The governments of Salazar and Franco had cooperated openly since the days of the Spanish Civil War. Yet Spain found itself ostracized for years by the Western powers, even by the early Truman administration; and it is still today excluded from

NATO, in spite of its bilateral military ties with the US. Portugal faced no such difficulties, however, in spite of its dictatorship at home and its oppressive colonial rule.

But then Spain had attracted much attention, and aroused much hostility, during its Civil War. People in Europe were much aware of Spain, and of its close ties with the Axis powers, despite its official neutrality in the war. Salazar had come to power in a less conspicuous way; the military coup which enabled him to take over had had few if any international repercussions. So, 'rightly or wrongly, it [Salazar's dictatorship] is regarded as less obnoxious than Franco's' (Arthur Whitaker, *Spain and the Defense of the West*, p. 287). In addition, the nature of Portugal's domestic policy was blurred by its close international relationship with Great Britain, and, most particularly, by the grant of the use of the Azores for the final stages of the war. Salazar seemed to slip quite easily from the close ties to Germany in the thirties, through neutrality, into the congenial context of postwar anti-communism.

With military considerations soon uppermost in the minds of postwar American policy-makers, and with the Azores cast for an important role in this global military planning, the inclusion of a dictatorship in an alliance for the defence of 'democracy' did not seem strange. As Adolf Berle put it, after bewailing the average citizen's failure to understand such issues, the logic goes like this:

> For example, you go to attend a session at the Air War College, attended by the highest air officers charged with American defence. These men know that air defence of the United States is impossible unless the United States is in some sort of international arrangement giving the Air Force ready use at least of the geography needed for their air bases and interception system (naturally, since their air squadrons may start in Kansas, refuel in Iceland, the Azores or Africa or Germany, thence to proceed on their mission). They know that this means building a system of foreign relations to match.

(*Tides of Crisis*, p. 8)

The military necessity to protect the Atlantic pointed to the inclusion of Iceland, and of Portugal's Azores Islands, in the

NATO defence network. So, although Salazar expressed his reservations on the democratic ideals expressed in the text of the treaty, Portugal became a member of NATO. The moral qualms which seemed to apply to Spain were deemed inapplicable, and no one of consequence raised any objections to the invitation extended to Portugal by the US and the Brussels powers. On 4 April 1949, the North Atlantic Treaty was signed, and American commitments to Portugal embodied in a formal treaty.

It should be pointed out that the treaty was limited to the North Atlantic area, thus excluding all colonial possessions except those of the French in North Africa. In theory, then, this commitment was less far-reaching than that of 1943, in which the United States pledged itself to respect Portuguese sovereignty in all Portuguese colonies. And this loophole has been used in the sixties to facilitate verbal dissociation from Portuguese colonialism. Until 1961, however, there was little thought of even verbal dissociation.

In the interim between the end of the war and the formation of NATO, the United States had continued to use the transit facilities in the Azores on an *ad hoc* basis. The airport built on Santa Maria island (under Pan American Airways cover, so that Salazar could tell Hitler it was purely a commercial arrangement) was turned over to Portugal. Portugal had attended the International Civil Aviation Conference at Chicago in 1944 (the Soviet Union refused to attend because of the presence of Spain and Portugal), and at the end of 1945 a civil air transport agreement was signed between the US and Portugal. Use of the military airbase on Terceira continued, although Portugal was reluctant to grant permanent rights. The original agreement expired in 1946, and was extended for eighteen months; then again in 1948, for three more years.

Beyond the transfer of the airbase facilities and the training of Portuguese personnel in such skills as weather observation and communications, there was little significant aid to Portugal during the years before the formation of NATO and the Korean War, which loosened Congressional purse-strings. Portugal, however, participated as a matter of course (Spain was excluded) in the Committee of European Economic Cooperation, the first meeting of which was held in 1947. In 1948 Portugal presented its first request for ERP (Marshall Plan) aid. Other European countries took priority, and aid to Portugal did not begin until 1950. And even then, as can be seen in Table 2, purely economic aid was substantial only in 1950 and 1951. From 1954 to 1960, aid of this kind was minimal.

Table 2 *US Foreign Assistance to Portugal:*
Obligations and Commitments (Millions of Dollars)

	Economic (total)	Military (total)	Economic and military (total)
1950	31·4	—	31·4
1951	19·0	0·4	19·4
1952	—	10·2	10·2
1953	−0·7	71·5	70·8
1954	—	33·4	33·4
1955	—	53·0	53·0
1956	8·2	43·8	52·0
1957	4·6	27·1	31·7
1958	3·5	18·9	22·4
1959	2·6	16·7	19·3
1960	3·8	9·7	13·5
Total	72·6	298·0	370·6

Source: ICA, Office of Statistics and Reports. *US Foreign Assistance July 1, 1945 through June 30, 1960.*

Military aid began in 1951, at the time when the agreement on the Azores was renewed. Portugal had not made any request for military aid in the first year of the Military Assistance Program. In late 1950, a military assistance survey mission visited Portugal to assess defence needs. During 1951, General Eisenhower paid a visit and was welcomed with enthusiasm; personnel of the Military Assistance Advisory Group (MAAG) began to arrive; and the first military equipment was delivered. A new agreement granting more extensive base rights in the Azores was signed in September. The arrangements made with Portugal accorded well with Berle's recommendation of a foreign policy tailored to military needs. Elizabeth Roy, in a paper for the Institute for Defense Analysis, characterizes such arrangements as 'essentially payment for the right to use a base or facility' (*U S Military Commitments*, p. 37).

Even with military aid, the totals in Table 2 do not seem particularly great alongside total American expenditures ($22 billion for military assistance to all countries from 1953 to 1961; and $1½ billion for Turkey in the same period). However, when the military aid is compared to Portugal's own defence budgets at the time, it is clear that it has been of substantial significance (see Table 3). The cumulative contribution has meant that substantial portions of the Portuguese armed forces are American-equipped and American-trained.

Table 3   *American Military Assistance compared with Portuguese Defence Expenditures 1951–60*

	Total US military assistance (*millions of escudos*)	Portuguese defence expenditures (*millions of escudos*)
1951	11	1,553
1952	286	1,691
1953	2,002	1,975
1954	935	2,100
1955	1,484	2,224
1956	1,226	2,297
1957	759	2,391
1958	529	2,485
1959	468	2,820
1960	272	3,023

American aid went to equip the Portuguese Army, Navy, and especially the Air Force. But its orientation was then primarily European. Portugal's 'overseas provinces' (as they were renamed in 1951) received comparatively little. Altogether, it appears, less than $1 million went for such projects as the highway from the Benguela Railway to Chingola, the port at Lobito, or the runway in Vila Luso. Also directed to transport was an Export-Import Bank loan of $17 million, made in 1953 to Rhodesia and Portugal for the rail link from Rhodesia to Lourenço Marques.

Relations with Portugal continued to be peripheral but friendly. Brigadier-General Julius Klein, on a European inspection tour for the Senate, visited military assistance operations in every NATO country but Portugal and Iceland. But perhaps this neglect was simply because there were no problems in the relationship. Portugal was the only NATO country that shared the American enthusiasm for incorporating Spain into the organization. In 1956 the yearbook *The United States in World Affairs* observed that 'not everything was dark in the Western military-political picture. Cooperation between the United States and Portugal seemed especially good' (p. 24). That year two new bases (Montijo and Espinho) were made available for NATO use, and the Azores agreement was renewed again, to 1962.

Not only did American diplomats refrain from challenging Portugal's colonial policies or its dictatorship; they appeared to condone such policies. The American Legation in Lisbon was raised to Embassy rank in 1944; and the series of American Ambassadors who were stationed there, according to a Portuguese opposition observer, 'went around cultivating the friendship of the rich and sociable Portuguese and those local American and British businessmen who were always ready to confirm that Salazar is a benevolent despot' (António de Figueiredo, *Portugal and Its Empire*, p. 61). William Attwood reports that the US consuls in Angola and Mozambique in 1961 supported Portuguese colonial policies. And the importance of the MAAG in the American mission (MAAG had a staff of forty-five in 1958) insured a continuing bias towards military considerations. Altogether the insulation of American representatives from views opposing Portuguese colonialism seems to have been quite effective.

Portugal as Seen by American Policy-Makers

Those diplomats directly involved in relations with Portugal had, we have seen, the expected bias. The absence of an African Bureau in the State Department meant no pressure from such a source to raise embarrassing questions on colonialism. And the leadership at the top was not concerned to remedy the imbalance. Indeed the attitudes of Dean Acheson and John Foster Dulles, the two most important Secretaries of State during this period, were scarcely incongruent with the policies adopted.

Dean Acheson has become in recent years one of the most prominent apologists in the United States for the white-ruled states of Southern Africa. Concentrating his attention on attacking the United Nations sanctions imposed on Rhodesia, he has found time nevertheless to write an introduction to hardline Portuguese Foreign Minister Nogueira's book *The Third World*; and to comment as he did in April 1969 to the American Society of Newspaper Editors:

Hostile harassment with our help of three friendly countries in Southern Africa is still going on. . . . these acts of harassment and folly were designed in the United Nations to coerce Portugal into setting adrift territories over which it has had political responsibility for twice the time of our own country's independent life.

(*On the Rhodesian Question*, p. 29)

Such a stance is not the reactionary consequence of senility; it is consistent with positions taken throughout his career in public life. Acheson has consistently maintained that priority must be given to maintaining good relations with our European allies. He assailed Kennedy's 1956 Senate speech supporting 'the orderly achievement of independence' in Algeria. And in his newly published volume of memoirs, *Present at the Creation*, he gives us another glance at his feelings.

At the 1952 NATO meetings in Lisbon, Acheson had a chance to meet with an old school friend, Ambassador Lincoln MacVeagh, who had come to Portugal after giving 'invaluable help in the rescue of Greece from internal subversion and external attack' (*Present at the Creation*, p. 622). In a private meeting with Salazar, Acheson 'felt drawn to him as rarely on first meeting' (ibid., p. 627).

Acheson was Secretary of State from 1949 to 1953. And he has played an important role in foreign affairs, in and out of the State Department, both before and since that time. He was one of the men called in to evaluate the American involvement in Vietnam before Johnson's 'reversal' of policy, and still represents for many the greatest years of American foreign policy. The lauding of his memoirs is indicative of his standing. Rarely did a reviewer think to criticize his racism as well as to praise his use of language.

The position of John Foster Dulles was similar. It is best revealed by an incident that occurred in 1955. Following a state visit to the United States by Portuguese Foreign Minister Paulo Cunha, a joint communiqué was issued, in which Soviet allegations concerning 'Portuguese provinces in the Far East' were dismissed. Since India was already in dispute with Portugal about Goa, and Portugal was about to join the United Nations where it would be asked to report on its 'non-self-governing territories', this reference to 'provinces' provoked a strong negative reaction from Afro-Asian governments. In a press conference on 6 December 1955, Dulles was asked about this.

Q: Mr Secretary, does this Government regard Goa as a Portuguese province?
A: As far as I know, all the world regards it as a Portuguese province. It has been Portuguese, I think, for about 400 years.
Q: Mr Secretary, did you say 'province' or 'colony'?
A: Province.

Even in the strictly legal terms on which Dulles presumably based his answer, it had been a 'province' only since 1951. Since a similar question had already been raised with respect to the French colonies, and India's concern was well known, ignorance is not a very plausible explanation. It is clear that there was no significant inclination on his part for even verbal dissociation from Portuguese colonialism.

Chester Bowles might have been referring to Acheson, Dulles, and many of their colleagues when he observed:

the very suggestion that the day may come when the Atlantic nations may no longer take what they need from the natural resources of Asia and Africa will be dismissed by many as preposterous. . . . Many American and Western European policy makers still seem to assume that this state of affairs is part of the ultimate pattern of life, and quite beyond the reach of earthly forces.

(*Africa's Challenge to America*, p. 53)

American policy under Acheson and Dulles was untroubled by any doubts about the permanence of Portuguese colonialism.

The United Nations Takes Up the Issue

In 1955 this assumption might have seemed unshakeable, for Portugal had not yet entered the United Nations. This meant that Portugal had been spared some of the attacks suffered there by the other colonial powers. Bowles hopefully remarked in 1956 that now that Portugal was in the UN 'it will be possible to focus more international attention on a system that appears second only to the Union of South Africa in its harsh treatment of Africans' (ibid., p. 90). The fulfilment of this hope was not notable before 1961; but it is true that the issue was raised, and the United States was forced, from time to time, to take an explicit stand.

Portugal's admission came finally in a deal with the Soviet Union, by which each side in the Cold War gained a number of new members. In early 1956, the Secretary General sent a routine note to Portugal, reminding it of the obligation under the United Nations Charter to report on 'non-self-governing territories'. Portugal replied that it had no such territories, and debate centred for several years on whether Portugal was legally required to report on its 'overseas provinces'.

The issue was discussed in 1957 and 1958. The United States, Britain, China (Taiwan) and France maintained that each state was competent to determine whether it had territories falling in the category of 'non-self-governing'. In 1959 a committee was established, including India, Mexico, Morocco, the Netherlands, Britain, and the United States, to propose an interpretation of the Charter. The committee's report made a clear case for calling Portugal to account, concluding that in the case of territories geographically separate and ethnically or culturally distinct from the metropole, there was a *prima facie* obligation to transmit information. Moreover, a resolution was proposed naming the territories of Portugal which were presumed to fall under this principle. Although the United States had participated in the work of the committee, it abstained on both the general and specific resolutions; as did Italy, France, the Netherlands, and Britain. Both resolutions passed by large majorities.

The United States also abstained in 1960 on the Declaration on Colonialism, which proclaimed support for the self-determination of peoples still under colonial rule. The vote was 90 to 0 in favour, with the United States joined in abstention by Australia, Belgium, Britain, the Dominican Republic, France, Portugal, Spain, and South Africa. The abstention was decided by President Eisenhower, against the advice of the U S Mission at the United Nations.

Even more indicative of American attitudes, and much less celebrated, was the U S position on the Security Council elections for 1961. The African countries had proposed Liberia as a candidate for one of the seats. Liberia, as a conservative African country, and one possessing special ties with the United States, might have been expected to gain American support. Instead, the United States proposed Portugal for the seat. And only after fourteen ballots did the United States and Western Europe give up their insistence that Portugal should get the place. A compromise was reached by which Liberia would serve for one year of the two-year term, and then give way to Ireland for the second year.

Such support for Portugal clearly went beyond the necessary 'payments' for the use of the Azores. In fact, the Eisenhower-appointed Clay committee on foreign aid had already said that 'every effort should be made to reduce assistance to foreign countries in return for these rights, especially Spain and

Portugal, which are already more than adequately compensated' (Committee to Strengthen the Security of the Free World, *Report*, p. 18).

President Eisenhower himself summed up American–Portuguese relations when he visited Lisbon in May 1960. Commenting on the 'spirit of complete mutual understanding' in his talks with Salazar, he declared that 'there are no great problems between the United States and Portugal'.

3 The Emergence of Armed Struggle against Portuguese Colonialism

As long as all seemed quiet in Portuguese Africa, nothing would seriously challenge Portugal's colonial system and American support for it. The United Nations defined a trusteeship role for colonial powers, preparing their dependencies for self-determination. Portugal did not accept such a role even in theory; and Portugal's Western allies had no incentive to challenge this view, however anachronistic it seemed. Vague talk of what might happen in the distant future was of little interest to practical politicians. It was much easier to accept the conclusion that Portugal's African subjects were content in the multicontinental Portuguese state. If there was to be any impetus towards independence, it would hardly come from Portugal or the outside world. It would have to come from the African people themselves.

But even observers sympathetic to the cause of African nationalism saw little evidence of the protest, political organization, and nationalist sentiment apparent in the rest of Africa. Thomas Hodgkin, writing in 1956 in his *Nationalism in Colonial Africa*, found little to say about nationalism in the Portuguese territories, except to cite its 'apparent non-existence' (p. 17). The barriers built by Portuguese censorship and political repression created the illusion that nothing at all was happening before Angola exploded into violence in 1961. But the liberation movements which in the 1960s began significantly confronting Portuguese rule did not emerge from a vacuum. Nor were they the work of 'outside agitators', communists, and Protestants, whom the Portuguese quickly claimed as responsible for these attacks on their 'civilizing mission'.

African resistance began with the initial Portuguese conquest, which was not complete until after the First World War. In Angola, Mozambique, and even in small Guinea-Bissau, Portuguese military expeditions had to be sent to subdue resisting tribes. In Guinea, the last important stage of the conquest was marked by the campaigns of Teixeira Pinto from 1912 to 1915. But isolated disturbances continued. The area of Canhabaque was 'pacified' only by a two-month campaign in 1936, twenty-five years before the beginning of modern guerrilla warfare in the territory.

The pattern was much the same in Angola. The struggle of the Dembos area against Portuguese pacification persisted from 1907 to 1910. A 1913 revolt in the Bakongo country of northern Angola was blamed by the Portuguese on Protestant missionaries, setting an early precedent. The Bailundu of southern Angola were conquered only by a major military campaign from 1902 to 1904.

In Mozambique the war of Gungunhana against the Portuguese in 1895 ended three years later with the deportation of Gungunhana himself to Portugal, and southern Mozambique was largely under Portuguese control before the end of the century. But in the more distant areas north of the Zambezi River, sporadic resistance prevented full pacification until the second decade of the twentieth century. The Niassa and Cabo Delgado areas, where today guerrilla warfare is most intense, were occupied for the first time in 1908–12.

The history of these wars of resistance, and others too numerous to mention, is hardly more than two generations removed from the present liberation movements, and the memories are alive today. Such resistance failed, say African leaders now, not only because of the disparity in military strength between the Africans and the Portuguese, but also because the resistance was tribal and/or local in character. It was only the emergence of movements with a wider national character that could make possible a modern struggle for liberation. The roots of resistance go back to tribal and traditional soil. But the territorial focus of the struggle, the definition of the enemy and of the community that must be mobilized against him: these are determined by the fact of subjugation at the hands of the same colonial power.

Thus, while resistance as such goes back into the pre-colonial and tribal past, modern nationalism stems from those groups most exposed to colonialism: the relatively small group of Africans and mulattos living in the towns; those working on the docks or in the plantations; those succeeding somehow in getting an education. The pattern of development is then not different from that in the rest of Africa: the early protests against the abuses of the colonial system by those who were the 'assimilated'; the growing radicalization of this group and the development of ties with the urban workers; finally mobilization of the peasants who formed a majority of the population.

But if the general outlines of the development of nationalism are similar, the particular situation of Portuguese Africa made for radically different details. The relative underdevelopment of Portuguese Africa meant that those among whom nationalism first developed were correspondingly few in number, and increased slowly. Probably even more important, the incipient protest and cultural improvement groups that did emerge were quickly and ruthlessly suppressed. We cannot know, of course, what would have happened had they been allowed to grow and organize openly. What we do know is that opposition went underground and into exile, and was able to emerge into the open only when it was capable of beginning an armed struggle.

Those groups that did organize openly had short lives, being soon suppressed, or captured by the colonial regime. The Liga Africana, established in Lisbon in 1923, hosted in that city W. E. B. Dubois' Third Pan-African Congress. Although conservative in style, and composed only of educated Africans and mulattos, the Liga Africana stood nevertheless for unity of the African peoples against colonial rule. The advent of Salazar's regime at the end of the decade put an end to its existence.

Similar groups formed as social or mutual aid associations in the African territories themselves. The Liga Nacional Africana (Angola), the Associação Regional dos Naturais de Angola, and the Centro Associativo dos Negros de Moçambique were just a few of these organizations. And their fate is illustrative. Organized in 1948 as a literary discussion group which published a magazine called *Mensagem*, the Associação Regional dos Naturais de Angola was banned in 1950 after two issues of their magazine had been published. The Liga Nacional Africana (Angola), formed in 1929, consisted primarily of *assimilados*. As it moved in the 1950s to more contact with the masses of Africans, and began to widen its limited discussion and protest, its elected leadership was displaced by officers appointed by the governor-general of the colony. A similar process occurred with the Centro Associativo dos Negros de Moçambique; so that in 1963 Eduardo Mondlane could characterize such organizations as 'at best simply bourgeois social clubs, often called upon to shout their part in the militarized chorus of allegiance to Salazar' (in John A. Davis, ed., *Southern Africa in Transition*, p. 201).

More overt protest by workers or peasants met with a more ferocious response. In 1959 fifty striking dockworkers in Bissau were killed by the Portuguese, while many others were wounded and arrested. The date of the Pijiguiti massacre, 3 August, is commemorated each year by the nationalists of Guinea-Bissau. In the 'Guerra de Maria', in Angolan cotton-growing country, in February 1961, Africans launched a campaign against the forced cultivation of cotton, destroying crops and European property. The Portuguese counter-attacked in force; and hundreds, perhaps thousands of Africans were killed, in indiscriminate aerial and ground assaults against African villages. António Mariano, the leader of the movement, was mutilated and killed after his capture.

There are many other incidents of which little is known but that something happened, in a dock strike or a peasant protest. Mueda, in northern Mozambique's cotton-growing country, was the scene on 16 June 1960 of a similar event, known in some detail thanks to the eyewitness description of Alberto-Joaquim Chipande. In 1968 he told his story to the English journalist Basil Davidson:

Certain leaders worked among us. Some of them were taken by the Portuguese – Tiago Muller, Faustino Vanomba, Kibiriti Diwane – in the massacre at Mueda. How did that happen? Well, some of these men had made contact with the authorities and asked for more liberty and more pay. . . . After a while, when people were giving support to these leaders, the Portuguese sent police through the villages inviting the people to a meeting at Mueda. Several thousand people came to hear what the Portuguese would say. As it turned out, the administrator had asked the governor of Delgado province to come from Porto Amélia and to bring a company of troops. But these troops were hidden when they got to Mueda. We didn't see them at first.

Then the governor invited our leaders into the administrator's office. I was waiting outside. They were in there for four hours. When they came out on the verandah, the governor asked the crowd who wanted to speak. Many wanted to speak, and the governor told them all to stand on one side.

Then without another word he ordered the police to bind the hands of those who had stood on one side, and the police began beating them. I was close by. I saw it all. When the people saw what was happening, they began to demonstrate against the Portuguese, and the Portuguese simply ordered the police trucks to come and collect these arrested persons. So there were more demonstrations against this. At that moment the troops were still hidden, and the people went up close to the police to stop the arrested persons from being taken away. So the governor called the troops, and when they appeared he told them to open fire. They killed about 600 people. Now the Portuguese say they have punished that governor, but of course they have only sent him somewhere else. I myself escaped because I was close to a graveyard where I could take cover, and then I ran away.

(*The Struggle for Mozambique*, p. 117)

These incidents went unreported at the time in either the Portuguese or international press. As far as the world knew, everything was quiet in Portuguese Africa. But among the clandestine or exile nationalist groups these events only provided further evidence for the conviction that only organized violence could possibly dislodge the Portuguese. It was in Angola that the storm first broke.

Angola: Initial Explosion and Protracted Warfare

The events in Angola in early 1961 have been described as a 'sequential explosion', with the focus of action shifting rapidly from one part of the country to another. The 'Guerra de Maria' in Kasanje went unnoticed by the world, and had no immediate national or international implications. But on 4 February the raid on the central prison in Luanda coincided with the presence of large numbers of foreign journalists, gathered to report on the quixotic seizure of a Portuguese luxury liner by Captain Henrique Galvão, a Portuguese opposition leader (see Chapter Four). It was impossible to conceal the fact of the attack, or the indiscriminate reprisals taken against Africans by white vigilantes. The hope of the Movimento Popular de Libertação de Angola (MPLA) was to free a number of political prisoners, whom it was feared were about to be executed. The prisoners were not freed, but the violence served as a catalyst throughout Angola, and caused the United Nations Security Council to place Angola on its agenda for the first time.

It was evidently with the hope of forcing international action against Portugal, and thus provoking a collapse of the Portuguese colonial system, that the União de Populações de Angola (UPA) moved from a policy of peaceful protest in exile to a plan for violent action. UPA, which had its origin and main strength in northern Angola, was able to take advantage of adjacent and newly independent Congo to maintain contact with its militants inside Angola. On 15 March 1961, rebellion broke out over wide areas of northern Angola. Although coordinated to some extent by UPA militants, it was much more an unorganized popular outburst of violence than coordinated guerrilla warfare. Some hundreds of Portuguese on isolated farms and in small towns were killed, although Africans had no arms except machetes, a few stolen rifles, and some old muzzle-loading hunting guns. The ferocity of the African attacks put an end to the Portuguese myth of the 'happy native', although the Portuguese regime attempted to characterize it all as an invasion

CONGO

Luanda

ATLANTIC OCEAN

Benguela

Mocamedes

ZAMBIA

NAMIBIA
(SOUTH-WEST AFRICA)

Liberated and contested areas

Railways

2. Angola

from the Congo, or as a reversion to primitive savagery by Africans who then deserved to be hunted down like wild animals. The retaliation, by troops and vigilantes, did just that. Not confined to those areas which had rebelled, it touched sections of Angola hundreds of miles away from the initial outbreak of violence. Thousands of refugees began to pour into the Congo; and thousands more died on the way, or in bombed villages. Educated Africans, particularly Protestants, were rounded up and executed. To missionaries in Angola at the time, it appeared that the Portuguese were determined to wipe out all present and potential African leadership.

The explosion came before the Angolan nationalist leadership was prepared for sustained military action. Among the UPA leadership in the Congo, the belief that Portugal was weak, the precedent of Belgium's abrupt retreat from the Congo, and a hope of action by the United Nations and Portugal's Western allies had led to expectations that the limited violence would shock Portugal into beginning to deal with the realities of African nationalism. The leadership of MPLA, scattered in prison, in exile in various African countries, and without secure access to the key base area in Congo (Kinshasa), was also unprepared as yet for a long-term guerrilla war. Portuguese retaliation, however, and the refusal of Portugal's allies to act against her, soon made it clear that independence could only come from a more prolonged military struggle.

In 1961 and 1962 a number of observers toured rebel-held territory in northern Angola. Although their governments continued to support Portugal, a number of organizations in the Western countries, and the newspaper-reading public, got some idea that there was a war on. But interest soon waned as events in the Congo overshadowed whatever was happening in Angola; and today many otherwise well-informed people, when one mentions Angola, comment, 'Oh, there was a revolt there some years ago, wasn't there?' The Portuguese for their part have lost no opportunity to announce periodically that the insurgency is 'under control'. The only scholars and newsmen who legally enter are those whose reports are unlikely to upset the Portuguese.*

At no time since 1961, however, has the situation really been 'under control'. The fighting has fluctuated widely, dependent in large part on political conditions in the neighbouring African countries, and on continuing divisions among Angolans involved in the struggle. But even at times when such circumstances have been most favourable for the regime, it has been unable to crush the activities of African guerrillas. Neither the presence of more than 50,000 troops, nor the token reforms intended to co-opt the more pliable among Angolans, could return Angola to pre-1961 'normalcy'.

For some years it seemed that UPA was the movement with the greatest chance of succeeding against the Portuguese. Operating from across the border in Congo (Kinshasa), and building on the fighting already begun, UPA by 1963 had sufficient reputation among African states to create a government in exile (GRAE), which was recognized by the Organization of African Unity. But the same factors which enabled some immediate successes contained long-range problems. The dependence on Congolese politics, which soon fell under predominantly American influence, ensured the linkage of UPA support, and arms supplies, to a country which backed Portugal as well. In 1970 GRAE was still dependent on American and other supplies funnelled through the armies of Morocco, Tunisia and Congo (Kinshasa). Under Mobutu, Portugal retains its representation in Kinshasa, and Portuguese traders are active in local Congo trade. GRAE's Congo base created another kind of problem as well. Precisely its strength among the Bakongo people inhibited its possibilities of gaining national support. Locked into a pattern of Western support and tribal politics, GRAE came increasingly into disfavour with the more radical African states.

*A recent exception has been the series of articles in 1970 and 1971 by Jim Hoagland, appearing in the *Washington Post*, which have presented a frank portrayal of the wars.

In contrast, MPLA faced greater practical problems in the early years of the struggle. Denied effective access to Congo (Kinshasa), communications with its guerrilla units functioning in the Dembos area north of Luanda were extremely hazardous. Actually expelled from Congo (Kinshasa) in 1963, MPLA, operating from Congo (Brazzaville), was forced to concentrate operations on the small enclave of Cabinda. Only in 1966, with the opening up of the Eastern Front, adjacent to Zambia, was MPLA able to mount military operations over large areas of Angola. (At about the same time, Jonas Savimbi broke away from GRAE and formed UNITA, which has carried on guerrilla action in some areas of eastern and southern Angola.) Since that time, MPLA has expanded the military struggle to ten of the fifteen districts of Angola, ranging from Cabinda to Cuando-Cubango in the south. Organization of administration, education, and health services in the liberated areas has expanded. With the expansion came a visit by the Military Commission of the Organization of African Unity, which withdrew (in 1968) official recognition of GRAE's status as a government in exile. MPLA, which had begun in Luanda, continued its organizing there, as indicated by the 1969 hijacking of a military plane flying from Luanda to Cabinda. The slogan adopted by MPLA in 1967 called for the Generalization of the Armed Struggle over the Whole National Territory. The struggle that began in 1961 continues, and is still expanding.

Guinea-Bissau: Successful Revolution in a Small Country

The Partido Africano da Independência da Guiné e Cabo Verde (PAIGC) had been organized in 1956. It was headed by Amilcar Cabral, a Cape Verdean trained as an agronomist who, during his studies in Lisbon, had been in close touch with Africans from Angola and Mozambique such as Agostinho Neto (of MPLA) and Eduardo Mondlane (of FRELIMO). The movement was first organized clandestinely in the capital, Bissau, and had its principal support among urban workers; its leadership came from the group of *assimilados* who formed a

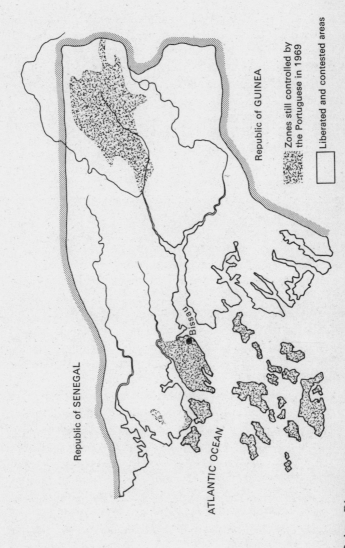

Republic of GUINEA

▦ Zones still controlled by the Portuguese in 1969

☐ Liberated and contested areas

Republic of SENEGAL

Bissau

ATLANTIC OCEAN

3. Guinea-Bissau

larger proportion of the population than in the two larger Portuguese colonies. It advocated complete and immediate independence.

Organization of urban workers resulted in several strikes, the most important of which involved dock workers in Bissau. This was suppressed by Portuguese troops, in August 1959; and in the following month the party decided to prepare for an armed struggle. The preparation involved above all the mobilization of the peasants, and the training of the militants who would be able to lead the struggle.

The contrast with Angola is clear. Although the Angolan movements had come to the conviction that violence was necessary, they had at first no systematically worked-out plan, and little political or military preparation for the struggle that was to follow. In Guinea, with the benefit of the Angolan experience, two years elapsed between the decision to initiate armed struggle and the first sabotage attacks in mid-1962. In the interim an effective organization had been established, inside Guinea and with international contacts. The PAIGC played an important role in the creation in 1961 of the Conferência das Organizações Nacionalistas das Colonias Portuguesas (CONCP), which attempted to coordinate the action of nationalist movements in all the Portuguese colonies. Arms and military training were arranged in North Africa and Eastern Europe. Despite the arrest of party organizers in Bissau, the network of organization extended itself throughout the country.

Guinea is a small country, sandwiched between Senegal and Guinea-Conakry. With the consistent support of Conakry and limited cooperation at least from Senegal, PAIGC was able to develop the armed struggle quite rapidly. In 1963 systematic guerrilla action began in the south, where dense forests and numerous waterways made the military situation favourable for the guerrillas. By mid-year the Portuguese Minister of Defence was admitting that guerrillas had infiltrated fifteen per cent of Guinean territory. Later in the year, a second zone of operations was created in the north. By the time of the first full party congress, which took place inside Guinea in February

1964, it was already necessary to give systematic attention not only to the organization of further military action, but to the political and economic administration of the liberated territory. Schools, medical services, trading posts, and a systematic effort to raise production of rice and other crops were early priorities. Although the number of Portuguese troops rapidly increased from ten to twenty-five thousand (some thirty-five thousand in 1970), by 1965 half of Guinea was included in the liberated zones. Attacks on Portuguese bases supplemented the earlier guerrilla tactics of ambush and sabotage. In 1966 a third front was opened in the east of the country.

In 1967 an attack was carried out for the first time on the central airbase at Bissalanca, only ten kilometres from the centre of the capital. The colonial economy of Guinea, based on the export of peanuts and on a trade monopoly by the Companhia União Fabril, had been substantially paralysed. On the islands of Cape Verde, Portuguese repression of nationalist forces intensified, but PAIGC reported that clandestine activity continued. There was as yet no armed struggle there.

By 1970 PAIGC claimed control of more than three fifths of Guinea. The Portuguese still had command of the air, which meant, as also in Angola and Mozambique, that the liberated areas were not exempt from aerial bombardment or Portuguese counter-attack. But these areas did serve as bases for military action against the remaining territory under Portuguese control. Rice production increased substantially, while exports of such products as palm oil helped pay for the import of necessary trade goods. More than a hundred nurses served in clinics in the interior, and the number of students enrolled in PAIGC primary schools approached 20,000. More advanced educational programmes were carried on at the PAIGC school in Conakry.

The Portuguese still hold parts of Guinea, along the coast, and in a section of the interior plateau. Their air and naval power makes it possible for them to continue maintaining communications with the outside, and even stage an occasional formal visit by a Portuguese dignitary. But the cost of maintaining even this limited control is high: 35,000 troops is approximately half the number in Angola, a colony almost twenty times the size of Guinea. In Guinea-Bissau Portugal has already found its Vietnam.

Mozambique: The Beginnings of a Long Struggle

Mozambique, even more than other Portuguese colonies, has exported its workers year after year to surrounding countries, and the first nationalist movements were organized among such exiles. Three separate movements took shape among Mozambicans in Rhodesia, Malawi, and Tanganyika.* UDENAMO (União Nacional Democrática de Moçambique) was organized in Rhodesia in 1960. MANU (Mozambique African National Union) was formed in East Africa along the models of the Tanganyikan and Kenyan parties TANU and KANU. UNAMI (União Africana de Moçambique Independente) was organized in Malawi. With the independence of Tanganyika in 1961, all three parties set up offices in Dar es Salaam.

Encouraged by CONCP, and by African leaders such as Nkrumah and Nyerere, the three movements merged in 1962. In the first congress of the new movement FRELIMO (Frente de Libertação de Moçambique), Mozambicans from the three parties, with a number of recent exiles fleeing from arrest in Mozambique, worked out a programme of action. Dr Eduardo Mondlane was elected the first President. The congress set a programme of political organization, the training of cadres, mobilization of world opinion, and the preparation of 'all requirements for self-defence and resistance of the Mozambican people'.

As was the case in Guinea, two more years elapsed before it was possible to begin the armed struggle. It was necessary to set up a coordinated clandestine organization inside Mozambique, to send men for military training (the first group of 250 was trained in Algeria); and to procure arms. It was also necessary to deal immediately with the lack of skilled personnel for even the most basic tasks, since Mozambique, and especially

*Now Tanzania.

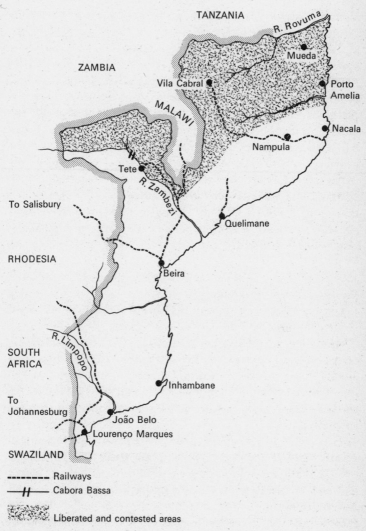

TANZANIA

R. Rovuma

ZAMBIA

Mueda

Vila Cabral

Porto
Amelia

MALAWI

Nacala

Nampula

Tete

R. Zambezi

To Salisbury

Quelimane

RHODESIA

Beira

R. Limpopo

SOUTH
AFRICA

Inhambane

To
Johannesburg

João Belo

Lourenço Marques

SWAZILAND

-------- Railways

⊦⊦ Cabora Bassa

Liberated and contested areas

4. Mozambique

the northern part, had suffered even more from the lack of education than had Angola. Mozambique's Protestant missions were fewer than in Angola, and restricted largely to the south; and the effects on African education were apparent. FRELIMO accordingly began educational programmes among the refugees in Tanzania, and sent large numbers of students on scholarships abroad.

The war began on 25 September 1964. Attacks were launched in four provinces of Mozambique: Niassa, Cabo Delgado, Zambézia, and Tete. It soon became clear that it would be impossible to continue supplying the units in Tete and Zambézia, and these were withdrawn to the other two northern provinces, where fighting escalated. In 1965, a British journalist, writing for two Rhodesian newspapers, reported on his visit to Niassa province with the Portuguese army. He commented that 'the FRELIMO, a Viet Cong in miniature, are a tough and elusive enemy. They generally operate in very small units, often of only half a dozen men.... They are at home in the jungle and bush, where they live off the country, striking silently by night, withdrawing swiftly into the dense cover if the Portuguese reply in strength.'

During the next three years FRELIMO continued this kind of war. Soon many of the guerrillas were being trained in camps inside Mozambique, and wide areas of the countryside were controlled by the movement. By 1967 FRELIMO had approximately 8,000 troops trained and equipped, not counting the militia or those trained men for whom there were as yet no arms available. Portuguese forces in the colony had risen to some sixty thousand.

From 1967 to 1970 FRELIMO forces in Cabo Delgado and Niassa provinces moved to larger-scale attacks on Portuguese posts and airbases. Mueda, the site of the massacre years before and now one of Portugal's major air bases in the area, was hit several times; one attack, in 1968, destroyed twelve planes on the ground. Heavier weapons and more experienced fighters, as well as the control of base areas inside Mozambique, made possible such intensification of the combat.

In the liberated areas, production of food crops increased, while the forced cultivation of cotton was abandoned. People marvelled at having enough to eat. Some cash crops such as cashew nuts and peanuts were cultivated, and traded by FRELIMO across the border for farm tools, cloth, and other necessities. FRELIMO nurses and medical aides set up a system of first-aid posts and clinics; primary schools were set up inside Mozambique and in the refugee camps. Administrative structures for the liberated areas were established.

But until 1968 FRELIMO seemed unable to push the fighting further south. This provided an opportunity for the Portuguese to play on the latent tension between northerners and southerners, and the contradiction between those who understood the necessity of a protracted war of liberation and those who expected an immediate victory. In March 1968 a new front was reopened in Tete province, adjacent to Zambia; a front of crucial strategic importance because of Portuguese and South African plans for the huge Cabora Bassa hydroelectric project. In July 1968 the second party congress, held inside Mozambique on this occasion instead of in Dar es Salaam, solidified the direction and the unity of the movement.

But the Portuguese launched another kind of attack. For it seems all too likely that it was they who arranged for a bomb to be mailed to Eduardo Mondlane, the President of FRELIMO. On 3 February 1969, he opened a package marked 'book', and was instantly killed as the bomb exploded. Mondlane had been central in setting FRELIMO's direction, and in holding it together. Western observers, attributing the assassination to internal party conflict, predicted that FRELIMO might well fall apart, and the Portuguese even re-establish control over the FRELIMO-dominated areas of Mozambique.

But that prediction did not come true. Despite a period of confusion and some discouragement, the direction corresponded less to Portuguese hopes than to a statement published by FRELIMO in its bulletin *Mozambique Revolution* shortly after the assassination:

This murder will be avenged and the enemies of the Mozambican people must expect our revenge to fall on them and their sons with inflexible justice. It was a vain hope they nourished if they thought to discourage us by this barbarous elimination of one man, even if a great man. In this they showed their weakness, their ignorance of the Revolution which has taught us through the toughest experience how to make of every apparent setback a new point of attack, how to use every momentary retreat as an opportunity for a run and leap forward, how to find in defeat the means for victory. We grow stronger from our calamities, and this case is no different from the other battles. It is a test for us, perhaps one of the harshest, but we shall face it with the kind of determination that the man we lost symbolized to us. . . . It will be another step toward independence. We will make it so. Because we will be more determined, more stubborn and implacable than we ever were. We will proceed with obstinate perseverance along the path of the Revolution and we multiply our efforts now that we have to fill that place made empty by murder.

Since 1969, FRELIMO action has continued to expand. The new Portuguese commander-in-chief in Mozambique, General Kaulza de Arriaga, has stepped up Portuguese action, and talks of success. But a *New York Times* report of 26 July 1970, from Lourenço Marques, comments that 'the new Portuguese offensive can change the nature of the war in Mozambique but is not likely to have a decisive influence on the course of events, in the view of independent military observers. These sources believe that the Portuguese have misjudged the strength of FRELIMO, overestimated the repercussions of the murder of its leader, Eduardo Mondlane, in February 1969, and underestimated the force of his successor, Samora Machel.' Reports from FRELIMO indicate that both on the military front and in such areas as the organization of education and health, the revolution continues to advance.

Portugal's 'Civilizing Mission' and Counter-Insurgency

Portugal's counter-insurgency efforts in Africa have followed, with variations, a course similar to that followed by the United States in Vietnam. A military effort based on aerial superiority, 'search and destroy' tactics, and the regroupment of the civilian population in 'strategic hamlets', has been accompanied by token or paper reforms intended to co-opt as many Africans as possible into accepting the Portuguese mission, and presence.

Such reforms have officially abolished the forced cultivation of cotton and other crops; emphasized education for Africans; and granted Portuguese citizenship to all, rather than just the assimilated. As already indicated,* however, these have not led to basic changes in the system. The peasant cotton farmer still bears the same relationship to the Portuguese companies which buy his cotton, and there are no effective checks on the authority of the local administrators whose responsibilities include the curbing of idleness. Formal citizenship is still accompanied by differential rights for those who before were the 'civilized' and those who were the 'non-civilized'; with different identification cards making the categories easy to distinguish.

But, above all, the primacy of white Portuguese interests, and of Portuguese power, has not been abandoned at all. Even in Portugal democratic command of government policy can scarcely be said to exist: much less in Africa. Immigration of Portuguese settlers continues to be encouraged. And the attempt to co-opt African support takes place in the context of a military struggle which, as in Vietnam, takes priority over any political considerations, and involves attacks on the civilian population as well as the armed guerrillas.

The military effort, moreover, has proved an increasing strain on Portugal's resources, financial and human. By 1970 the total number of Portuguese troops in Africa was estimated at about 160,000, or more than double the 1964 level. In proportion to Portugal's population, this is a troop level more than five times that of the United States in Vietnam at its highest. The new military service law, passed in early 1968 and revised in 1969, increased the period of military service to two years overseas, plus whatever other time was spent in training or in Europe.

*Chapter One.

And demobilized troops may be recalled for up to twenty-eight months. Women and cripples have also been made eligible for military service in support positions. Meanwhile the flight of young Portuguese workers to France has continued, in spite of prohibitions on leaving the country.

Portugal's defence budget has soared, and for 1968 was estimated at some 10,000 million escudos ($350 million), or more than triple the 1960 budget, and almost half the total budget for the year. Nor does this figure include the separate budgets of the 'overseas provinces' for military appropriations. The possibility of financing such an increase by normal fiscal measures has become increasingly difficult. Portugal's foreign debt by 1966 already amounted to six billion escudos, compared with 510 million in 1961. Military aid from Portugal's NATO partners and from South Africa has been a help; but not nearly as much as Portugal requires.

A continuing and escalating war can be financed by the country only through continued economic growth, and this means increased foreign investment. Restrictions placed on investment in the 'overseas provinces' have accordingly been relaxed, and there has been a notable influx of foreign capital, particularly in Angola, but also in Mozambique (see Chapters Six and Seven). Special taxes are levied to support the war effort.

Thus, escalating guerrilla action has so far been met by a parallel expansion of the Portuguese military apparatus, and of the economic basis to support that apparatus. How long such a pace can be maintained is an open question. Such discoveries as that of oil in Cabinda by Gulf Oil Company seem calculated substantially to increase Portugal's resources. But manpower is another matter. The population of Portugal is only ten million, and the use of African troops is limited by their political unreliability. The labour shortage has already had a significant effect on wage increases in metropolitan Portugal.

Some profess to see the replacement of Salazar by his old associate Marcelo Caetano as a significant step towards reform and accommodation with African interests. But the extent of reform so far has been a small loosening of the bolts on free speech in Portugal itself; while for the 'overseas provinces', Caetano has only proposed some increases in administrative autonomy. Those who would benefit from such changes are primarily the white settlers. There has been no sign that Caetano is planning any significant concessions to African rule; and he has proclaimed his determination to continue the war to keep the 'overseas provinces' Portuguese. Those in the liberation movements do not expect significant change. Caetano's regime depends on the same military and economic elite that supported Salazar.

4 American Policy Under Kennedy and Johnson: Image and Contradiction

As we have seen, before 1961 there was in effect no American policy towards Portuguese colonialism. But the times were changing. Britain, France, and even Belgium decided that granting independence gave them the best chance of holding on to some influence in their colonies. The United States encouraged them in this opinion, realizing that it opened up new opportunities and responsibilities in Africa for the United States. The old slogans of self-determination were trotted out, along with talk of America's anti-colonial heritage. Of the American Presidential candidates in 1960, Nixon had visited Africa in 1957, and warned on his return of the 'battle for men's minds' in that continent. Kennedy had, as long ago as 1956, called for a policy in the United Nations more sympathetic to colonial peoples, and had spoken out for Algerian self-determination in 1957. The crisis in the Congo at least brought Africa to the attention of the American public, although the portrayal seemed to highlight the dangers of 'premature independence'. With the Congo, Cuba, and Laos in the news, Europe seemed less a priority, and the 'Third World', the new battlefield for power and influence.

So the general context of American policy had changed substantially by 1961. The specific situation in Portuguese Africa was to change even more radically during that year: from apparent tranquillity to armed revolt. The new American administration had to reconsider conventional policy. And the world was to be given an opportunity to see just how far the United States would really go in supporting self-determination in Africa.

The Santa Maria, *Angola, and the United Nations*

Four days after Kennedy's inauguration, a Portuguese cruise ship in the Caribbean (the *Santa Maria*) was captured by an anti-Salazarist group headed by Henrique Galvão. Galvão had been a colonial administrator in Angola in the 1940s, and had prepared a report condemning the forced labour system there. Since then he had been part of the Portuguese opposition: at times in jail, most recently in exile. His plan was to seize the ship and make his way to Angola, with the eventual goal of a revolution that would overthrow Salazar and install General Humberto Delgado, an opposition leader who had run unsuccessfully for President in 1958. As with many other anti-Salazarist Portuguese, Galvão advocated reforms in the 'overseas provinces', but opposed independence and African nationalism as vigorously as he did Salazarism.

The *Santa Maria* affair may have been 'the symbolic beginning of the end for Portugal in Africa' (James Duffy). It was also a unique stunt which confused the international lawyers and captured the attention of novelty-seeking journalists. A small group of men had captured a luxury liner. The Portuguese government was crying 'piracy', and the American Navy was embarrassed by its inability for days to locate the captured vessel.

On 23 January, the day after the capture, a formal request for rescue of the ship from piracy was made by the Portuguese Foreign Ministry to the United States. The Navy sent two destroyers to intercept the vessel 'under the well-defined terms of international law governing piracy and insurrection aboard ship'. A State Department spokesman said that the Navy 'will take such measures as are necessary and appropriate to reinstate the control of the ship by constituted Portuguese authorities'. It seemed that the US government accepted completely the Portuguese version of 'piracy', rather than Galvão's assertion that the seizure of the ship was part of an insurrection against Salazar, a domestic affair among Portuguese in which other nations should not interfere. By 25 January, when the *Santa Maria* was finally spotted by a Navy plane, the position was much more confused.

First of all, the 'well-defined terms of international law governing piracy' had evaporated. When Robert Kennedy called the State Department and asked to speak with an expert on piracy, he found that no one really knew anything about it. Boarding the ship and forcibly restoring the control of the Portuguese authorities no longer seemed so unambiguously justified. Moreover, there were American passengers on board; and while it seemed that all were unharmed, it was impossible to predict what might happen should the Navy launch an attack against the *Santa Maria*. For more than a week after his ship was spotted, Galvão negotiated with the Navy, while the Portuguese government fumed. Finally a landing in Brazil was arranged for 2 February. The passengers were released, and the next day Galvão and his companions received asylum from Brazil's newly inaugurated President Jânio Quadros.

The Portuguese government was patently distressed that the United States had deigned to negotiate with Galvão, and had delayed so long the recovery of the ship. On 30 January a spokesman in Lisbon accused the United States of failing to live up to NATO obligations. Hints were dropped reminding the United States of Portuguese generosity in allowing the use of the Azores base. Even though the Portuguese were eventually satisfied – the *Santa Maria* was turned over to Portugal by the Brazilian government – the incident had 'irritated the Portuguese government to no small degree against the new administration in the United States, which displayed more interest in assuring the safety of the *Santa Maria*'s passengers than in upholding the Salazar regime' (*The United States in World Affairs: 1961*, p. 125).

The American reaction to the *Santa Maria* incident might well serve to illustrate American policy on Portugal for the next nine years. The United States had other interests than those of Portugal (in this case primarily the safety of American passengers), and was not willing entirely to subordinate its policy to Portuguese political interests. Portugal, understandably, was not pleased at being reminded that it did not automatically have top priority. But on the other hand the US Navy did prevent Galvão from reaching Angola, and the ship did get returned to Portugal. There was no serious challenge to Portuguese interests, and Portugal had no real grounds for complaint. Much the same pattern was observed as a quixotic rebellion on the high seas was followed by full-scale revolt in Africa. US action upset the Salazar regime, but turned out to involve no real break with Portugal and its colonial policy.

Events in Angola, as we have seen, followed closely on the stunt by Galvão. As white vigilantes joined in the reprisals against Africans in Luanda, Liberia requested an urgent meeting of the Security Council. In the meeting of 15 March, a draft resolution was introduced, calling on Portugal to introduce reforms in conformity with the previous year's resolution on the Granting of Independence to Colonial Countries and Peoples. The Security Council resolution also mandated a sub-committee to study the situation. The resolution failed, with no negative votes, but with six abstentions against five positive votes. Latin American and European countries abstained, but the United States voted in favour.

The American vote was widely taken as 'the harbinger of the new attitude on colonial affairs generally' (*The United States in World Affairs: 1961*, p. 33). Backed by the American Mission at the United Nations, by the new State Department Africa team of Mennen Williams and Wayne Fredericks, and such higher State Department officials as Chester Bowles and Harlan Cleveland, the initiative was also supported by the President himself. According to Richard Walton, then Voice of America correspondent at the United Nations, the State Department establishment and the 'foreign policy crowd' in Washington and New York might still see the world through the eyes of cold warriors; but 'Kennedy himself and some of his top advisers were more sympathetic to the Third World' (*The Remnants of Power*, p. 111). African leaders themselves began to expect some positive action. Holden Roberto, whose followers attacked the Portuguese in northern Angola on the same day that the Security

Council voted, praised the Kennedy administration for its vote.

Stevenson, in his speech to the Security Council, deplored the violence on all sides, but spoke particularly about Portugal's obligations:

The United States would be remiss in its duties as a friend of Portugal if it failed to express honestly its conviction that step-by-step planning within Portuguese territories and its acceleration is now imperative for the successful political and economic and social advancement of all inhabitants under Portuguese administration – advancement, in brief, toward full self-determination.

Portugal felt abandoned, and was particularly enraged that the United States had chosen to vote on the same side as the Soviet Union. Anti-American demonstrations were held in Luanda and in Lisbon, and accusations were made of a world-wide conspiracy against defenceless Portugal. Portugal denied the legal right of the United Nations to interfere in a purely internal matter, and rejected any resolutions based on the assumption that its overseas provinces were 'non-self-governing'. Moreover, Portuguese spokesmen maintained, any threat to the 'maintenance of international peace and security' came not from Portugal, but from outside terrorists, openly supported in their aggression by the Afro-Asian states. Portugal was portrayed as the innocent target of attacks from international communism; and as defending Western Christian civilization by its presence on three continents. It was an incomprehensible shock that the United States, the leader of the world-wide anti-communist crusade, should desert so loyal an ally.

In Angola the fighting continued. Reports of the savage Portuguese reprisals reached the outside world through refugees fleeing to the Congo, and through expelled Protestant missionaries. On 20 April the General Assembly passed resolution 1603(XV): by a vote of 73 to 2, with 9 abstentions. This, repeating the one introduced in the Security Council the previous month, called on Portugal to implement self-determination. Portugal was asked to abide by the resolution of 1960 which demanded the 'transfer [of] all powers to the peoples of those territories, without any conditions or reservations, in accordance with their freely expressed will and desire, without any distinction as to race, creed, or colour, in order to enable them to enjoy complete independence and freedom'. In 1960, the United States had abstained on that resolution. This time, the American vote was in favour.

In June the Security Council met again, this time adopting a resolution by a vote of 9 to 0, with only 2 abstentions. It deplored 'the large-scale killings and the severely repressive measures in Angola'; called on Portugal to act in accord with the General Assembly resolution; and demanded that 'the Portuguese authorities desist forthwith from repressive measures'. The hope was expressed that a peaceful solution could be found. The United States again voted in favour of the resolution.

Standing Still and Moving Backwards

If United Nations resolutions had remained on the level of generalities, then continued American support might have been forthcoming. But within the United Nations, Portuguese intransigence was seen as a provocation, and more serious action was demanded. The Special Committee on Territories under Portuguese Administration completed its report in August 1962. After a careful examination of Portuguese policy prior to 1961, and of the purported reforms during that year, it declared that 'the danger lies, on the one hand, in Portugal's insistence that there can be no change in its relationship with the Territories, which it considers are integral parts of its national territory, and, on the other, in the complete disregard for the legitimate aspirations of the indigenous populations.' As representatives of the African nationalist movements had expressed willingness to negotiate with Portugal over the terms and timing of independence, the Committee concluded that the onus for the lack of any peaceful solution by negotiation fell on Portugal, which refused to consider the possibility of independence. The Committee also concluded that the arms furnished to Portugal by her allies were of aid to her in suppressing the people of Angola. It therefore recommended that the General Assembly 'should consider and adopt measures aimed at the immediate discontinuance of such assistance and a complete embargo on further sales and supplies of such weapons'.

The initial American position in the UN had been a symbolic one. The operative provisions had simply called upon Portugal to change her policies; and a committee had been established. To make even such a symbolic break with Portugal had taken the direct support of President Kennedy. Since then the continued debate within the administration had led to a 'moderating policy on Portuguese questions in the UN'. Arthur Schlesinger comments that 'we labored to tone down the Afro-Asian assaults on Portugal; that was why, as Stevenson tried to explain to Acheson, we took part in the drafting of resolutions' (*A Thousand Days*, p. 562). Acheson had opposed even this.

But the resolutions coming before the General Assembly in December 1962 moved from general disapproval, the language of which could be toned down to the point where the US would accept it, to a call for specific sanctions against Portugal, namely an arms embargo. For the US to approve such a resolution, and abide by it, would be a major new departure. Even had all those who in 1961 pushed for US approval supported the further step, it would have required a major Presidential initiative to override the opposition in the State Department and Pentagon. That initiative was not forthcoming.

In the realistic terms so congenial to Kennedy, the pay-off from such a step could hardly outweigh the disadvantages. On the one hand there would be increased prestige with the African states – prestige that was not always translatable into influence – and a remote hope that Portugal might thereby be shocked into moving towards independence for its colonies. On the other hand, there might follow the loss of the Azores, and, at the least, increased Portuguese resentment, discontent among America's other European allies, and political repercussions at home. A recent study of American foreign policy notes that 'any desertion of an ally, for whatever reasons, would be regarded by many Europeans as evidence of American inconstancy and susceptibility to sentimentality and non-European pressure' (Gerberding, *United States Foreign Policy*, p. 187). According to Sorenson, Kennedy 'finally felt that, if necessary, he was prepared to forgo the base entirely rather than permit Portugal to dictate his African policy' (*Kennedy*, p. 538). But Kennedy was even less interested in following the strong Afro-Asian line. He shared Stevenson's anger at the Indian take-over of Goa in late 1961. According to Schlesinger, even if it had not been for the Azores, it is likely that the United States would have continued to pursue a 'middle course'. Kennedy wanted 'not hortatory resolutions against colonialism, but realistic resolutions which could lay the economic, educational and institutional foundations for self-government' (*A Thousand Days*, p. 563). How such resolutions could have had any effect in the absence of a Portuguese response is not clear.

Schlesinger admits that 'similar language ... had long been used by the white man as a pretext to deny the Africans their independence. But again the spirit of Kennedy in his personal talks with African leaders rescued the language from its old context and made it the expression of thoughtful concern and friendly counsel.' In so far as this was successful, it seems largely to have been a politics of image, or illusion; the attempt to build identification with the Third World, while avoiding the steps which might alienate Portugal even further and open Kennedy up to political reprisal from Republicans and from more conservative European-minded Democrats. From 1962, the United States abstained on or voted against all major resolutions concerning Portuguese colonialism.

By 1964 the gap between the African position and the American one had widened even further. On 25 September 1964, the Mozambique Liberation Front began guerrilla activities in Mozambique; and Portugal was faced with war in all three colonies. The same year also saw American military aid to Tshombe, now installed as leader of the Congo, who faced rebellion and sought to suppress it with the aid of white mercenaries and American air transport. The United States flew Belgian paratroopers to Stanleyville (by way of the Azores) to rescue hostages held by rebel troops, and to allow Tshombe's forces to capture the town. What Americans saw as a humanitarian 'rescue mission' was seen in Africa as a political move, dictated in part by the Western assumption that the lives of whites were worth more than the lives of black Africans. It became more and more natural to link the other Western powers, and particularly the United States, with Portugal, rather than to regard Portugal as only an anachronistic exception.

In the United Nations, the Special Committee on Decolonization appointed a sub-committee to study the activities of foreign economic interests in non-self-governing territories. The ensuing report in 1965 concluded that such interests were directly or indirectly supporting Portuguese colonialism; and that, together with the government of Portugal, they bore the responsibility for the sufferings of the people in the territories. The General Assembly resolution of 1965, adopted by 66 votes in favour to 26 against, reiterated the previous demand for an arms embargo, and went on to ask states to 'prevent activities of their nationals in economic interests impeding the attainment of freedom and independence in the Territories'. As if to confirm the importance of such economic factors, Portugal in 1965 significantly liberalized the restrictions on foreign investment in the 'overseas provinces'. Since then outside involvement has increased substantially, while UN reports have documented the involvement, and resolutions have continued to condemn it.

The United Nations resolutions have accumulated over the years, and African guerrillas and Portuguese troops continue an as yet inconclusive conflict. But US policy remains stuck in the position set by the end of 1962; and, on such an issue, to stand still is to go backwards. The United States continues to express general support for self-determination in Portuguese Africa, and occasionally votes in favour of a resolution which condemns Portuguese incursions across the border of Congo or Zambia. A trickle of support is given to students and other refugees, whom, it is hoped, will show their gratitude to the US if they ever become the leaders of independent countries. The United States continues to oppose, however, any action involving an embargo on arms to Portugal, or any limitations on 'foreign economic interests'.

Pressures for the Standstill Policy

The initial steps taken by the United States in 1961 can be seen, in retrospect, as having had little impact in moving Portugal towards compliance with self-determination. They seemed more important at the time because they were taken by many as evidence of American willingness for further dissociation from Portugal and fuller identification with African aspirations. In the dramatic atmosphere of 1961, it seemed not impossible that the United States would abandon her NATO ally, whose contribution to NATO was not that great after all, and throw its weight on the side of African independence. Such a hope was doomed to disappointment. Both the immediate pressures and the basic assumptions on which American policy was built worked against such a radical change.

One of the steps taken by Portugal to strengthen her position in the United States was to hire a public relations firm, Selvage & Lee. The contract was arranged in April 1961 by the Overseas Companies of Portugal. Formed in March 1961 at the instigation of the Portuguese government, this group involved approximately fifty Portuguese and foreign businesses operating in Angola and Mozambique. The duties of Selvage & Lee were 'to publicize via newspapers, radio, television and otherwise the accomplishments of Portugal in its overseas provinces. Also, to combat with facts in all available media false and misleading information relating to the present strife in Angola.'* The close relationship between the Portuguese government and the Overseas Companies is revealed by the fact that Selvage & Lee

*Information on the Selvage & Lee contract is available in Hearing before the Committee on Foreign Relations, United States Senate (88th Congress, First Session) on Activities of Nondiplomatic Representatives of Foreign Principals in the United States.

reported to both, and close working relationships were established with Portuguese representatives in the United States. On 31 May 1961, James P. Selvage wrote to an official of Portugal's Overseas Ministry: 'We are working closely with your Ambassador to the United Nations and will do all possible to assist him in making a strong case for Portugal. Likewise, our Washington office is cooperating fully with your Ambassador to the United States.'

The assistance given involved both public relations and lobbying. One of the tasks was to get improved press coverage. During the visit later in 1961 by Assistant Secretary of State G. Mennen Williams to Angola, a Selvage & Lee representative, Fred Shaw, was assigned to deal with the press accompanying him, which included correspondents from NBC, Reuters, *New York Times*, Associated Press, and *US News and World Report*. In Shaw's report to Kenneth Downs, the account executive, he told of his success:

I set up my room in the Hotel Continental as a sort of press headquarters where we all met to discuss any problems, plans for trips, arrangement of interviews, and the general philosophy of the story they were down there to report. I must say here that all of these men were good, objective reporters, most of them pretty well schooled in African affairs. But since they had not before been allowed into Angola, a number of them had a chip on their shoulder against the Portuguese, and my first mission was to remove same. I believe the results show that this was successfully done, since not one prejudiced story was written during their stay and I believe every one of them left in a pro-Portuguese frame of mind. I might point out that this should pay off in the future in any writing or broadcasting they do on the subject of Portuguese Africa.

In January 1963 a special tour of Angola was arranged by Selvage & Lee for members of the Newspapers Editors Association, which represents editors of small daily and weekly papers. The majority of the group were quite impressed. James Z. Miller, editor of the *Washington Missourian*, wrote on his return: 'If Portugal is forced out of Angola within the next few years, and the country is turned over to the natives, the result will be far worse than the Congo ever was. There will be anarchy, rape, murder, and a general disregard for all law.'

One editor was not so impressed. Wayne Sellers, of the Rock Hill, S. C., *Evening Herald*, wrote in a letter home: 'We had 5 days in Angola and I was terribly upset by it all. I have never seen such blatant brainwashing and we free loaded through all of it, including terribly expensive lunches, dinners, cocktail parties, etc. . . . I am disturbed that many of our group seem to have fallen for it.' He was even more disturbed when he discovered that the trip had been arranged by a public relations firm.

The propaganda campaign concentrated on appealing to the anti-communist and racist sentiments of the American public. Wide use was made of reprints from the November 1961 *Reader's Digest*. One article, by Brig. Gen. Frank L. Howley, Vice-President of New York University, was entitled 'Reversion to Savagery', and talked of 'primitive, hideous terror', with a large element of communism behind it. Another writer, on retainer from Selvage & Lee, wrote a series of articles for the *Charleston News and Courier* which attacked the support given to African independence by American Negro leaders, declaring the 'inescapable conclusion' that such a movement was 'Negro-über-alles'. Later, Selvage & Lee tried to repudiate this particular article: for, as one of their representatives testified to the Senate Foreign Relations Committee, 'Well, if it becomes known that we sponsored material of this kind on behalf of the Portuguese, the Portuguese multi-racial policy is a sham and a fraud.' More common than explicitly racist propaganda was the attempt to portray the Africans as savages. A widely distributed pamphlet, entitled 'On the Morning of March 15', was composed primarily of photographs of atrocities purportedly committed by the terrorists in northern Angola. Selvage & Lee made a special effort to point out that 'the United Nations harangues and resolutions were based on racial hatred. The Afro-Asians, foolishly following the Communists, were relentlessly driving for a black Africa.'

Another tack was followed in a special section arranged for the *Pittsburgh Courier*, a leading Negro newspaper. Much emphasis was placed on the Portuguese 'multi-racial' policy of assimilation. The headline read 'Racial Integration Promoted for 500 Years'. George S. Schuyler, the Associate Editor of the *Courier*, noted that except where the terrorists had invaded, he saw in Angola 'peace, tranquility, order, and great industrial and commercial activity'. Other special attempts were made by Selvage & Lee to reach the Negro public, and the Moss H. Kendrix Organization, a Negro public relations firm, was employed for several months to help. Articles were placed in the Washington *Afro-American* and in *Jet* magazine, and several Negro journalists were given trips to Angola. It appeared, however, that such efforts had little effect. In late 1962 the American Negro Leadership Conference on Africa called for steps to ensure that no American weapons were used against Africans in Angola, and condemned the activities of Portugal in spending large sums of money to misinform and mislead the American public.

Much more intensive, and more successful, efforts were designed to use Portuguese-Americans, who could speak with special force on this issue, and who were concentrated in New England, where their political influence might sway a number of key Congressmen. A Portuguese-American Committee on Foreign Affairs was formed in October 1961, at the instigation of and financed by Selvage & Lee. It was headed by Dr Martin Camacho, a Portuguese-born lawyer from Boston, who in 1952 had headed the Portuguese-American Committee for the Election of John F. Kennedy (as Senator). Dr Camacho was active in sending letters to newspapers, making speeches, and contacting Congressmen. The 'Committee', which consisted of some seventy Portuguese-Americans, was in little evidence except on the organization letterhead; some members were not even aware of who was paying for the organization.

Among the results of Camacho's activities were a number of speeches attacking US policy. Kenneth Downs, of another public relations firm employed, reported:

I am sending Dr Pinto Basto (Chairman of the Board of the Benguela Railway) copies of the Congressional Record. You might explain to him that we wrote some twenty speeches. Joe Martin, Speaker of the House under Eisenhower, for example, used Sam's stuff without change, apart from abbreviation. You might point this out to Dr Pinto Basto and tell him that it required a great amount of work on the Hill to get the time allocated for these speeches. ... In all fairness Camacho should be given a great deal of credit on this one. It was his tireless pressure on some of the Massachusetts Congressmen that made it possible, and he is the one who at the last minute got Speaker McCormack into the act.

The speeches, by twelve Massachusetts Congressmen (and several from other states), were printed and distributed as a pamphlet by the Government Printing Office on the initiative of Representative Thomas P. O'Neill, Jr.* It was entitled *Friendly Relations Between Portugal and the United States – A Victory for Freedom.*

By January 1963 Dr Camacho could comment in a letter to his committee that 'since January 1962 we have observed a marked change in the official United States attitude toward Portugal. There is now an apparent willingness and disposition to listen to the Portuguese viewpoint on its African provinces.' By 1967/8, the firm (now Downs & Roosevelt, with the arrival of Kermit Roosevelt, former employee of the C I A and of Gulf Oil Company) had adjusted as well to the new emphasis on economic involvement. Its required report to the Department of Justice noted that

since the political climate in the United States as regards Portugal had sufficiently improved, and the image of Portugal in public opinion and in the press in this country had changed so much for the better ... the time has come for us to shift the emphasis of our work from political and general information to the areas of economic development, promotion of trade and investment, and work with the universities.

Portugal could congratulate itself on a successful public relations effort.

Something more than public relations, however, was involved in the improved political climate noticed by Downs &

*In 1971 Representative O'Neill became the new Democratic Party whip in the House of Representatives.

Roosevelt. In particular, the Azores bases, although their importance had been diminished by the increased range of modern aircraft, were regarded as essential by the military. They had been used in the 1958 intervention in Lebanon, in the Berlin crisis of 1961, and in the 1964 Stanleyville paratroop drop. In 1963 it was still true that 'approximately 75 per cent of normal U S military air traffic to Europe and the Middle East transits the air facility on Terceira Island, and this base would be indispensable in the event of an emergency requiring U S forces to be sent to those areas' (Deputy Assistant Secretary of Defense Frank K. Sloan, quoted in *The Angolan Revolution*, p. 273). Dean Acheson reflected that the Azores bases were 'perhaps the single most important (set of bases) we have anywhere' (*Yale Law Review*, Autumn 1961).

In the summer of 1961 the Joint Chiefs of Staff had declared the Azores essential to American security in the event of trouble over Berlin. Thus Portugal had considerable leverage to apply by threatening not to renew the agreement. Since December 1962, when the old agreement expired, the use of the bases has been continued on an *ad hoc* basis. No new agreement for any specific period of time has been signed, and Portugal retains thereby a strong bargaining point in its discussions with the United States.

But to say that Portugal was blackmailing the United States, and that this was the main explanation for American policy, would be to confuse the issue, and certainly to obscure the role played by Portugal's friends *within* the American government. Among the military, both the Navy and the Air Force had a special interest in the Azores. And since Portugal was a member of N A T O, albeit a minor one, it had a special priority both with the Pentagon and with the Bureau of European Affairs in the State Department. This would have been true regardless of the particular status enjoyed by the Azores. If the Azores bases were used as blackmail, they were so used not just by Portugal against the United States, but by the Pentagon and the Bureau of European Affairs against those in the administration who thought African interests should have a higher priority. In the absence of special intervention by the President, the Bureau of African Affairs and the Mission to the United Nations could hardly hope to be a match for the 'Europeanists'.

For that group, it was not just the Azores that made Portugal important. As Acheson put it in 1958, relations with geographically and culturally close states are of first importance. 'Primacy must be given to maintaining confidence and trust in these relations. In our case, these states are those of the Western Hemisphere and Europe' (*Power and Diplomacy*, p. 62). According to George Ball, Dean Acheson's spiritual successor, the United States should 'recognize that Africa [is] a special European responsibility just as today the European nations recognize our particular responsibility in Latin America' (*The Discipline of Power*, p. 241). In November 1961 George Ball succeeded Chester Bowles as Undersecretary of State. Bowles, former Ambassador to India and the author of a book on Africa in 1955 when hardly anyone else of influence in the United States seemed interested, was the recognized advocate of a policy more sympathetic to Third World interests. After a subsequent year with a vague assignment as Special Representative and Adviser to the President for African, Asian, and Latin American Affairs, Bowles resigned. The victory of the Europeanists was clear.

Basic Factors Limiting Change in Policy

Even if more 'liberal' elements had won in the policy debate, there is good reason to believe that there still would not have been a radical break with Portugal. For the questions raised about Portugal touched on stances basic to America's position in the world: the importance of NATO, and American understanding of self-determination and revolutionary violence.

The North Atlantic Treaty Organization has consistently been regarded since its formation as the most important military alliance in which the United States is involved. Portugal itself might not be crucial to the alliance. But any withdrawal of support from her would raise questions about the alliance as a whole. The ascendancy of the 'Europeanists' in the State Department is built on the importance given throughout the postwar period to ties with Europe. The United States did not in 1961 or 1962, nor would it now, countenance action which, while attacking Portuguese colonialism, might cause a rift within NATO. The fact that the Azores base was especially dear to the military was only the most obvious part of an existing, functional, military tie. Strong incentives would be needed to convince policy-makers to chance disrupting such ties; and such incentives, in the terms of the policy-makers, have not appeared.

The conflict between the image demanded by the need to appeal to the Afro-Asian bloc, and the reality of the existing military alliance, is illustrated by the controversy over the use of NATO weapons supplied to Portugal. Accusations were made, in 1961, that weapons supplied for NATO use had been sent to Angola. At the time, the American Representative at the United Nations, Jonathan Bingham, denied the accusation. The following year it was admitted that the weapons had been used in Angola, but that (or so it was claimed) Washington had lodged a protest against such use. Portugal then gave an official assurance that arms supplied to it under the NATO agreements would not be used in the overseas provinces. The assurances have been unconvincing; but American policy continues to rest, at least formally, on the assumption that military aid to Portugal in Europe has nothing to do with Portugal's wars in Africa, and that therefore there is no need to break the NATO ties. (Chapter Five gives more details of American military ties with Portugal.)

Several assumptions about what kind of self-determination is legitimate have also set basic limits to American policy. Stevenson's Security Council speech of 1961 is revealing in this respect. In contrast to the resolution for which he voted, which called for immediate steps to transfer all powers to the peoples of those territories, Stevenson emphasized the danger of 'premature independence' such as that in the Congo. The problem there had been, he said, that 'the pressure of nationalism rapidly overtook the preparation of the necessary foundation essential to the peaceful and effective exercise of sovereign self-government'. On the one hand this meant that Portugal should be urged to undertake such preparation; this was the main point of the speech. On the other hand, it implied that as long as such preparations were not undertaken voluntarily by Portugal, it was important that the pressure of nationalism be curbed.

Indeed, either a precipitate Portuguese withdrawal or the expulsion of Portuguese influence by force would be, from the American point of view, undesirable. This conclusion is in turn built on two presuppositions.

The first is that self-determination should be of such a character that Portugal is able to maintain and develop its influence, and play an important role in the future of Portuguese Africa. As Undersecretary of State G. Mennen Williams put it, later in 1961, the fact that the US had not sided with Portugal in the UN votes 'did not indicate an American belief that Portugal should be forced out of Africa' (Department of State *Bulletin*, 27 November 1961). On the contrary: the assumption was that economic and other relationships, such as those between the British or the French and their former colonies, should be developed. In fact, the United States has consistently opposed the specific application of the word 'independence' as a goal for the Portuguese colonies. The argument has been that self-determination does not necessarily mean independence, but might well be the choice of such a relationship as that of the United States with Puerto Rico. The use of the word 'independence' would be to prejudge the issue, and to assume that Africans would not choose to retain a formal association with Portugal.

In 1963, Ambassador Stevenson, replying to the Portuguese Foreign Minister Nogueira in a Security Council debate, said, 'I hope he does not fear that any of us are seeking to deprive Portugal of its proper place in Africa.' The Department of State *Background Notes* on Angola are even more explicit:

The United States recognizes the contribution made in Africa by Portugal and believes that it is important that Portugal continue to contribute to stability in that continent. Because of the rapidity of change in Africa in the last decade, it believes that Portugal can continue to play a role in the continent only if it undertakes an accelerated program of reform designed to advance all the peoples of the territories towards the exercise of self-determination.

The United States, then, agrees that Portuguese influence should be maintained in Africa. The difference is over the means Portugal employs, which American policy-makers tend to regard as archaic and perhaps ultimately self-defeating.

The assumption that Portugal should be enabled to maintain her influence meshes well with the second basic presupposition of American policy: that the transition to self-determination must be orderly and peaceful. Thus Stevenson's speech in March 1961 condemned equally violence by all sides in Angola, and stated that further violence would only make constructive efforts more difficult. Such an even-handed condemnation of violence loses considerable credibility when one considers that it came only a month before the Bay of Pigs, and from the representative of a country that continues military relations with Portugal, or one party to the conflict.

It is undoubtedly true that the United States would have preferred, and would still prefer, an 'orderly, peaceful and rational accommodation' between the Portuguese and the forces of African nationalism. But the reason is clearly not opposition to violence as such. Closer to the point is the belief that 'strife, violence . . . and support for "national liberation" movements are the Soviets' best tools and the free world's greatest liabilities' (Arnold Rivkin, *The African Presence in World Affairs*, p. 244). Peaceful accommodation, on the other hand, would 'preserve and stimulate existing economic relationships beneficial to both the underdeveloped areas and the former European metropoles. These relationships could be integrated with new or expanded relationships with other free-world states' (Rivkin, *Africa and the West*, p. 59).

By this emphasis on a certain kind of peaceful accommodation, the realities of the situation in Portuguese Africa are obscured: that there is real rather than an illusory conflict of interest between African nationalism and Portuguese colonialism; and that it is Portuguese intransigence, with the absence of any peaceful options for political action, which has led Africans to employ violence.

The events in Goa in 1961 revealed graphically the divergent assumptions about the legitimate uses of violence held by American leaders and by Afro-Asians. In December, India, rejecting Portuguese sovereignty over Goa, and impatient with years of futile attempts to negotiate with Portugal, occupied the enclave by force. Asians and Africans viewed the move as a long-overdue elimination of an imperial remnant. They considered the use of violence justified by Portugal's intransigence in clinging to its colonial possessions. India stated: 'we cannot in the twentieth century accept that part of international law which was laid down by European jurists ... specifying that colonies in Asia and Africa which were acquired by conquest conferred sovereignty on the colonial Power.' The United States, and other Western powers, refused to admit that the colonial issue had anything to do with the question; for them it was simply territorial aggression. Stevenson proclaimed that 'what is at stake is not colonialism; it is a bold violation of one of the most basic principles of the United Nations Charter'.

The principle to which Stevenson referred is contained in article 2, paragraph 4, of the United Nations Charter. It states that 'all members shall refrain in their international relations from the threat or use of force against the territorial integrity or political independence of any state'. India and other anticolonial states maintained that Goa was not part of the Portuguese state, and that the use of force could not be considered a threat against Portugal's territorial integrity or political independence. As John Foster Dulles had done, Stevenson still regarded Goa as legally Portuguese territory. The same assumption it seems, is applied today to Portugal's African possessions. In the Department of State background notes on Portugal, the population is given as 22.7 million (or the figure that it would be if the African colonies were included); and the Portuguese terminology of 'overseas provinces' is accepted. In other words, the legal interpretation is based entirely on the *status quo*, in spite of United Nations determinations to the contrary.

Richard Walton, U N correspondent for the Voice of America, says that Stevenson was aware of the injustice of a speech that attacked only the Indian action without condemning as well Portuguese colonialism. He had been instructed, however, by the State Department (at Salazar's request), to delete any reference to Portuguese colonialism. Yet the passionate bitterness of Stevenson's attack on India revealed his own feelings as well as compliance with instructions. He spoke dramatically of witnessing the first act in a drama that could end only with the death of the United Nations. He reminded his listeners that 'the League of Nations died when its members no longer resisted the use of aggressive force'. He attacked the hypocrisy of India. There was Indian hypocrisy, of course. Indian advice to other nations on the need to avoid the use of force had become proverbial. Yet to anti-colonial nations it seemed significant that the representative of the United States (hardly a pacifist nation), and a man who was to defend so soon afterwards the Bay of Pigs assault on Cuba, should have reacted so strongly when force was used against European colonialism.

But the most important inference to be drawn from this episode is not just American hypocrisy. It is that the United States regarded as illegitimate the use of force against Portuguese colonialism. Its counsel to India, and its counsel to Africans today, is patience in the face of intransigence. As U S Ambassador Seymour M. Finger put it in the 1969 U N debate: 'while such peaceful change remains possible – however slow it may be – we are convinced that such peaceful means are in the best interests of everyone concerned.' Given American support for Portugal, the effect of advice to Africans to have patience and refrain from violence is to allow the monopoly of violence to remain with the established colonial government, with its police and armed forces.

The American position, then, although not entirely pleasing to Salazar, stopped short of any significant break with Portugal – even in the days of the 'New Frontier'.

Persuading Portugal to Reform

One of the standard American replies to criticism of its obstructive role in the United Nations is to claim that the United States has been active in persuading Portugal to reform. Strong resolutions, the U S argues, would make such communication more difficult; impatience with Portugal, and intemperate language, must therefore be curbed. Instead of attacking Portugal and employing sanctions, the United Nations should await the results of persuasion.

This approach is, if judged precisely in terms of results, obviously a failure. Portugal continues to reject even the possibility of independence, and war continues in all three African colonies. But serious doubts can also be raised about the seriousness of the American proposal. For those charged with communicating to Portugal the necessity of accepting self-determination have hardly been energetic in doing so.

In late 1961, immediately before the Indian occupation of Goa, Secretary of State Dean Rusk had met at the N A T O meeting in Paris with Dr Franco Nogueira, the Portuguese Foreign Minister. 'At no point did the Secretary express any reservations about permanent Portuguese control of Goa or even acknowledge that the Indians might have a legitimate point in resenting the Portuguese presence' (*A Thousand Days*, p. 526). The United States had asked India to postpone action for six months, and pledged diplomatic pressures meanwhile. The Indian judgement seems to have been accurate in attributing little significance to such a pledge. India was a major ally of the United States, and could not count on the most rudimentary diplomatic support against Portugal. Africa could hardly expect more.

In other American contacts with Portugal, it even seemed that the American representatives were more eager to transmit the Portuguese case to the United States and the world than any support for the African case to the Portuguese. In August 1963, George Ball relates, he 'flew to Lisbon, as a personal representative of President Kennedy, for a quiet visit with Prime Minister Salazar to review the problems of Portuguese Africa' (*The*

Discipline of Power, p. 246). His discussions, in which he was much impressed by Salazar, resulted in 'no meeting of the minds between our two governments'; but 'it did help to clear the air'. He accepts uncritically Portuguese propaganda that 'the leaders of the insurrectionary movement are predominantly from two tribes, each of which is an unpopular minority within its own territory'. And the basic requirements he suggests for a solution include: (1) 'a tough-minded but not unsympathetic understanding of her [Portugal's] problems and responsibilities'; (2) 'the precious element of time'; and (3) 'economic assistance' – for Portugal, of course.

Ball concludes that . . .

the real danger, of course, is that after a long war of attrition in which her overseas territories were devastated from one end to the other, Portugal would collapse. And the longer the struggle continued, the more likely that the Soviet Union and perhaps China would try to fish in troubled water. . . . the situation, in its very nature, would not be in the best interest of the United States or its Western European allies, since Angola and Mozambique are extensive and strategically important territories, lying at the heart of Africa.

(*The Discipline of Power*, p. 251)

No more than in the reflections of George Kennan or Dean Acheson years before, does any hint emerge from George Ball that the peoples of Angola and Mozambique might have any role to play in their own future. Nor does it seem that he approves even of the UN resolutions for which the United States had voted. On the contrary, he hopes that Western nations will 'relinquish their roles of detached but self-righteous critics' of Portugal.

Such opinions are, of course, consistent with Ball's viewpoint on the supreme importance of Europe in American foreign policy. That his quiet visit with Salazar should be presented as evidence of a sincere attempt at persuading Portugal to change course can only be regarded as laughable.

Certainly America's ambassadors to Portugal, who have the continuing responsibility of diplomatic communication, have been no less 'assimilated' to the Portuguese point of view. Charles Burke Elbrick, ambassador from 1958 to 1963, had been in Lisbon before, from 1940 to 1943; he was a career diplomat. For a time during the Eisenhower administration, he had served as Assistant Secretary of State. In accounts both of the *Santa Maria* incident and of the Goa debate, he was a special pleader for the Portuguese point of view. In an action reminiscent of Kennan's commitment in 1943, he promised Salazar that Portuguese colonialism would not be attacked in the UN debate on Goa. And the promise was kept. As late as 1961, his subordinates, the US representatives in Angola and Mozambique, were maintaining the Portuguese point of view at the Addis Ababa conference of American diplomats in Africa.

The ambassadors appointed by Kennedy and Johnson gave little indication of being any different. Kennedy's appointment was Admiral George W. Anderson, Jr, removed as Chief of Naval Operations because of conflict with McNamara. Clearly, the dispatch of a military man to the post indicated that the priority of military matters in the relationship with Portugal was to be continued. In 1964 Admiral Anderson visited Angola and Mozambique, and was honoured in Lourenço Marques with a banquet given by Governor-General Sarmento Rodrigues, also a Navy Admiral. Admiral Sarmento Rodrigues expressed his delight at the visit, since now his friend Admiral Anderson could appreciate that 'the Portuguese nation is not confined to its European territories, for it is exalted principally in the "overseas" lands, in which are situated its chief values and responsibilities' (*Presença de Moçambique*, v, 3, p. 278). On his return to Portugal Admiral Anderson addressed the American Men's Luncheon Group in Lisbon. He said that his visit had made him understand the problem of the Portuguese in Africa; and, although he was in no position to discuss political or internal policy, he had been impressed by the 'civilizing presence' of Portugal overseas.

Johnson's appointment of William Tapley Bennett, Jr, seemed even less felicitous. Bennett had previously served in Greece from 1961 to 1964; immediately prior to his appointment to Portugal in 1966, he had been ambassador to the Dominican

Republic. In the Dominican crisis of 1965 he had from the first identified with the regime and against the rebels who wanted to restore the constitution. Tad Szulc, in his book on the Dominican invasion, quotes one high Washington official as saying that 'Tap didn't seem to know anyone who was to the left of the Rotary Club,' and that in the revolt he 'almost reflexively gave his full commitment to people he knew' (*Dominican Diary*, p. 67). There is no evidence that he has changed since arriving in Portugal. In March 1969, rounding up his visits to 'overseas' Portugal with a trip to the Cape Verde islands, he congratulated the Portuguese on their multiracial policy, and commented that 'this visit has left us with the best of impressions'.

In April 1969, Ambassador to the UN Seymour M. Finger, continuing his argument that peaceful change, no matter how slow, was in the best interests of all, pleaded:

> Let us not proceed obstinately with tactics of the past – of repeating year after year resolutions which are known to be ineffectual on the day they are adopted – of adopting resolutions based on myths such as the red herrings of foreign military bases and foreign economic involvement. Such outworn shibboleths cannot substitute for the hard thought we must all give to the solution of the remaining hard-core problems. Though it may appear elementary to say so, it would also be wise not to slander those countries whose cooperation is considered important to achieving the objectives of resolutions to be adopted.

Richard Walton served as correspondent at the United Nations for the Voice of America, and observed the continuing debate on Portuguese Africa. His comments are a fitting reply to Mr Finger:

> Unrealistic, according to the United States and a few other major industrial nations, are resolutions that ask these countries to take actions matching their words. The United States and a few others are eloquent in speeches proclaiming their devotion to national freedom and racial equality, but when the smaller nations ask them to demonstrate their support by taking action against the racist governments in South Africa or Rhodesia or against Portuguese imperialism, the resolutions are invariably described as unrealistic. Unrealistic they

are indeed, primarily because the United States, Britain, France and a few others are the only nations that can make them effective, and there is not a chance in the world of their sacrificing their own economic or military interests even to a modest degree to support the Afro-Asian position although, even by their own definition, it is the just and honourable one. ... The United States would like the UN to be silent as well as powerless.

(Richard Walton, *The Remnants of Power*, p. 203)

It is not that the United States refuses to support the resolutions because they are unrealistic; such resolutions are unrealistic because the United States refuses to support them. They call for the relinquishment of military and economic ties with Portugal which the United States is unwilling to relinquish. And that is why Africans in Portuguese Africa have increasingly recognized that they fight not only against Portugal, but against a whole imperial complex headed by the United States.

5 Military Support for Portugal

On the face of it, the rhetoric of self-determination would seem to preclude close military ties with Portugal. 'Not so,' respond American diplomats. The argument goes something like this:

American relationships with Portugal and NATO have nothing to do with the wars Portugal is fighting in Africa. NATO is a purely defensive alliance whose territorial boundaries are confined to Europe and the North Atlantic. Its concern is exclusively the defence of Europe. Moreover, there are no such things as 'NATO' arms; arms are produced by individual countries, not by the alliance. That one ally may sell or give arms to another member of the alliance does not make those arms 'NATO' arms. Charges which seek to implicate NATO in Portugal's colonial wars are therefore misdirected: based on ignorance and prejudice.

Moreover, the bilateral American military relations with Portugal deal exclusively with American and European defence. Maybe in 1961 Portugal did use American equipment, allocated to NATO use, in Africa instead; but now Portugal gives assurances that new equipment received is for use only in Europe. Therefore it's not necessary to have an arms embargo. In fact, such an action would constitute an illegitimate interference in the right of the North Atlantic nations to organize for self-defence.

Indeed, Europe is not Africa. Unfortunately, the Portuguese do not agree.

Portugal's Military: Organized for Colonial Repression

Even if it were true that no newly supplied American weapons are being used by the Portuguese in Africa, the American argument would still depend on the assumption that the role of Portugal's military in Europe is quite separate from its role in Africa, so that cooperation in one area has nothing to do with cooperation in the other. That assumption is false.

It is false, first of all, because the Portuguese make no such clear distinction. The mission of the armed forces is the defence of the national territory. The national territory includes, by definition, the 'overseas provinces'. At present the chief preoccupation of the Portuguese armed forces is, of course, Africa. Portugal is fighting no other wars. The whole character of the defence establishment is moulded by its 'mission' overseas.

A look at Portugal's military budget confirms that, for the Portuguese, Europe and Africa are militarily inseparable. The accounting is so mixed that it is impossible to distinguish what money goes where. Each territory has its own armed forces budget, and Portugal herself has not only an 'ordinary' defence budget, but also a budget for 'extraordinary' defence expenditures. The budget of each territory includes both receipts from local taxes and from the central government. And the central budget, both ordinary and extraordinary, includes expenditures relevant to the whole of the 'national territory', and for all three forces (Army, Navy, and Air Force).

The deployment of Portuguese forces also defies a clear-cut division between Europe and Africa. Of an estimated 1969 total of some 180,000 troops, only some 18,000 are assigned to NATO; while approximately 150,000 are in Africa. A given unit in the Army generally serves two years 'overseas', and then is rotated back to Portugal. Although the law provides that the normal term of military service is for two years, the recruit usually spends time in uniform both before and after his time in Africa. A major function of the Navy, and to some extent of the Air Force, is transport between Europe and Africa. Of the Air Force, only one anti-submarine reconnaissance squadron is assigned to NATO. Both Navy and Air Force have regional commands in metropolitan Portugal and overseas.

The Portuguese military also play an important political role. Salazar came to power as a result of a military coup, and throughout the four decades of his rule the support of the military has been one of the key bulwarks of the regime. Caetano was chosen as his successor only when it was known that he was acceptable to the military. The armed forces have grown since 1961, and their influence, with their special interest in the colonies, continues to be crucial. Even those wishful thinkers who see Caetano as a 'liberal' recognize that he is severely limited in that role by the ultra-right factions in the military. To them it is of particular importance that no concessions towards abandoning the 'overseas provinces' be even considered. In the 'elections' of late 1969, one of the many restrictions was one against candidates discussing the wars in Africa.

The military works in close conjunction with other control agencies: the PSP (Polícia de Segurança Pública); the GNR (Guarda Nacional Republicana); and the General Directorate of Security (the new name for the infamous PIDE). On 19 January 1970, the Portuguese Minister of Army and Defence, General Sá Viana Rebelo, stated that the fundamental objectives of the Army in Portugal were the maintenance of 'internal security and public order'. The colonial wars, too, are 'internal security', for Portugal's 'overseas provinces' are considered part of one 'unitary nation'. This is the mission of the military establishment which since 1951 has had the friendly advice of an American Military Assistance Advisory Group.

American Military Aid to Portugal

Military aid to Portugal, since its beginning in 1951, has never been large compared to the quantities dispensed around the world, and especially in Vietnam or Taiwan. And in the 1950s it was less than the aid given to more important countries in Western Europe. But now, among European countries, it is exceptional. The United States has devoted major efforts to encouraging Western Europe to pay its own way in defence. By and large, the effort has been successful. Now only Portugal and Spain continue to benefit regularly from the Military Assistance Program. In 1959 the Clay Committee expressed the opinion that the two countries had already been adequately compensated for American bases on their territory. Aid to them could have been phased out. It was not, in spite of Portugal's growing involvement in three colonial wars.

The precise figures on aid given are difficult to obtain. Sources differ, and money allocated for a given year may represent deliveries spread out over several subsequent years. The following figures are from the Statistics and Reports Division, Agency for International Development; they represent actual deliveries during the indicated fiscal years.

Table 4   *U S Assistance to Portugal (Millions of Dollars)*

	Military Assistance program	Total Military	Economic
1949–52	10.6	15.6	51.2
1953–61	270.1	301.4	27.4
1962	4.4	5.8	69.1
1963	8.7	9.3	7.4
1964	5.6	6.1	16.5
1965	7.5	7.6	7.0
1966	1.5	1.7	5.9
1967	2.2	4.6	10.9
1968	3.2	3.7	7.2
Total 1962–8	33.1	39.1	124.0
Total 1949–68	317.9	349.0	202.8

The level of aid in 1969 and 1970 is approximately $1 million per year. It is unlikely to change substantially unless a new agreement on the Azores is negotiated with the Portuguese. The aid given, although a help to the Portuguese military, is less than they would like, and renegotiation of the bases agreement might provide increased contributions. The agreement with Spain in August 1970 included a provision for $300 million of aid over a period of five years, and was concluded by the Nixon administration over the objections of the Senate Foreign Relations Committee.

According to General Lemnitzer, testifying in 1968 before the House Committee on Foreign Affairs, American aid to Portugal 'is designed to train key Portuguese military personnel and to provide maintenance support material'. Up to the end of 1963, a total of 2,288 Portuguese military men received American training; there were 205 in the period from 1964 to 1968. In 1969 and 1970 approximately 130 are undergoing training.

Some of the training takes place in Portugal, and is carried out by the Military Assistance Advisory Group, of twenty-five men. Others are brought to the United States for special training, in such fields as communications/electronics, maintenance, administration, and missiles. It is claimed that the number of Portuguese receiving training at Ft Bragg, the counter-insurgency school, is small: not more than five in all. In fiscal year 1970 there was one Portuguese officer studying psychological warfare and counter-insurgency at Ft Bragg. An American officer at Ft Bragg, Col. W. L. Hinton, was sent in January 1970 to the Army's language school to learn Portuguese for subsequent assignment to Portugal.

Material support, in the form of equipment, is given to the Army's NATO division, to the Navy, and to the Air Force. The NATO division is equipped with American-supplied M-47 tanks, 105-millimetre and 155-millimetre guns, trucks, jeeps, and other technical machinery and vehicles. The light weapons and munitions for the Army are largely manufactured in Portugal from NATO patterns. In 1961, it was admitted later, equipment from this NATO division was used in Angola. Since then, American officials state, Portugal has given assurances that equipment supplied for this division will not be transferred to Africa. Responsibility for checking that this provision is not violated rests with the American Military Assistance Advisory Group.

The contribution that the United States makes to Portugal's Navy has been the loan of two destroyer escorts since 1953 (the loan was extended in 1967), and the recent contribution of three new destroyer escorts, the last of which was completed in 1969. More substantial additions to the fleet are being built in Portugal, France, and West Germany. The Navy is essential to the colonial war, for maintaining communications and transporting troops and supplies. The whereabouts of the American-supplied vessels is not reported in the Portuguese *Revista de Marinha*; so it is not clear whether they have served in Africa or not. The British, however, were given similar assurances, and two frigates supplied by them have spent most of their time in Angola and Mozambique. In the case of ships from France and Germany, no effort is made to maintain the pretence, and the *Revista de Marinha* (June 1969) speaks openly of their intended use overseas.

The Portuguese Air Force, although now receiving German and French aid, still has many American planes. These include 50 F-84 Thunderjets; 50 F-86 Sabrejets; C-47, C-54, and DC-6 transports; several hundred T-6 and 30 T-37C trainers; some 20 B-26 bombers; 18 PV-2 Harpoon bombers; and 12 P-2V Neptune bombers. Only the Neptune bombers are assigned to NATO. Of these planes, the official American position is that the majority were supplied before 1961 (which is true), and that none of those supplied since then are being used in Africa (which is not true).

Edgar Cardoso, in an official publication of the Portuguese Aeronautics Secretariat (*Presença da Força Aérea em Angola*), described the aircraft used in 1961 against the rebel attacks. He refers to the use of the F-84 and PV-2 for 'offensive support' of ground troops; to the use of the T-6 for 'armed reconnaissance'; and to the use of the C-54 for transport of troops and paratroopers. The T-6 trainer, converted to anti-guerrilla use, has served as the work-horse of the war overseas. American in origin, it is also on sale now in other countries; most recently Portugal is reported to have been buying models from France.

On 17 May 1964, at the Alverca air show in Portugal, a squadron of F-86 Sabrejets, for the entertainment of observers, displayed its proficiency with napalm bombs and rockets (*Revista Militar*, June 1964). After a new sale of F-86s to Portugal by West Germany, accusations were made that they were being used in Africa, particularly in Guinea-Bissau. The United States, which under the contracts retains responsibility for planes sold by a recipient to a third country, denied the accusations. In 1967, however, the American representative at the United Nations stated that the F-86s 'previously stationed in Africa had been withdrawn at the request of his government'. Also appearing at the Alverca show were a number of T-37C trainers recently received from the United States. A training aircraft, the T-37C is especially equipped for anti-guerrilla warfare, and has been used in Vietnam. It is not known whether these particular planes are being used in Africa; pilots trained in them undoubtedly serve in Africa.

The United States does not bother to deny that other planes, such as the C-47 and C-54 transports, or the F-84 fighters, are being used in Portugal's colonial wars. Although five new C-54s were supplied to Portugal in 1965, most of the planes are from before 1961. But the planes already supplied do have to be maintained. The majority of the work is done in the Portuguese Oficinas Gerais de Material Aeronáutica, which also does maintenance work on American planes in Europe, and has facilities for work on all the planes used in the Portuguese Air Force. It strains the imagination to believe that parts going into planes headed back to Africa are carefully separated out, so that no parts bought from or supplied by the United States could possibly end up there.

The NATO Alliance and Portugal

American cooperation with Portugal is set within the wider context of the NATO alliance. In the United Nations the United States has made much of the fact that the legal boundaries of the NATO area do not include the Portuguese possessions in Africa. Therefore, NATO has nothing to do with wars in Africa. Portugal, however, does not agree. Responding to attacks on the use of Fiat G-91 jets from West Germany in Africa, a Portuguese Foreign Ministry spokesman gave this interpretation:

The transaction was agreed within the spirit of the North Atlantic Pact. It was agreed that the planes would be used only for defensive purposes within Portuguese territory. Portuguese territory extends to Africa – Angola, Mozambique, and Portuguese Guinea.
(*Flying Review International*, April 1966, p. 459)

Nor is a 'strict' interpretation of NATO's territorial limits always agreed to by American military men. A handbook on NATO prepared by USAF Brigadier-General Monro Mac-Closkey, who served with the NATO command, points out that 'the definition of the military area in which the Treaty is applicable in no way implies that political events occurring outside it cannot be the subject of consultations within the Council' (*NATO*, p. 27). On 6 May 1963, the Commander of Allied Forces in Europe, Lyman Lemnitzer, while on a visit to Lisbon, was somewhat more specific. He said: 'Portuguese soldiers, while fighting for the defence of principles, are defending land, raw materials, and bases, which are indispensable not only for the defence of Europe, but for the whole Western world.'

In more concrete terms, Portugal derives from NATO a number of continuing benefits. One is a detailed review, updated annually, which 'leads to comprehensive exchanges of views on the overall problems facing countries in the defence field and to a multilateral discussion based on the full and detailed information supplied by each member country concerning the state of its forces, future defence plans, and its economic and financial situation' (*NATO Handbook*, 1965, p. 41). More specialized consultations are also held, such as the annual meeting for Study of Ammunition and Light Weapons (the May 1966 session was held in Lisbon). Portugal by now produces most of the light weaponry she uses; consultation with NATO countries ensures that she keeps abreast of new developments, and adjusts production to NATO standards. NATO standards are also applicable to much equipment sold bilaterally to Portugal from Belgium, Germany, or Italy. Mercedes-Benz, for example, advertises in the Portuguese *Jornal do Exército* its 'Nato-model' trucks – and sells them as well (see Chapter Seven).

The NATO Defence College in Rome admits fifty students

per six-month term, for upgrading the officer corps of the member nations. Portuguese officers attend along with officers from other N A T O countries. Other special courses are arranged at N A T O level or bilaterally. One such course open to N A T O countries involves training in chemical and biological warfare, at the V I L S E C K school in West Germany.

A recent list of officers promoted (in the *Jornal do Exército*, September 1968) illustrates the type of background that Portuguese officers have. One, just transferred to Mozambique, had completed a N A T O course in cryptography. Another had spent time at the Command Staff College in Fort Leavenworth, Kansas, at the Headquarters of the American First Infantry Division in Germany, and then in Angola. A third had gone from N A T O to the Portuguese General Staff in Mozambique and then back to N A T O. The result of this pattern is not only that the Portuguese officers 'maintain a broad outlook and are up to date in military developments and techniques' (*Military Review*, August 1964), but also that officers from other N A T O countries learn about what is happening in Africa – from the Portuguese point of view.

It is symbolic of N A T O sentiment towards Portugal that in 1967 Portugal's status in the alliance was upgraded. The N A T O Atlantic Command Headquarters is in Norfolk, Virginia. But when N A T O offices had to move from Paris as a result of the French withdrawal, advantage was taken of the reorganization to put into effect a plan to establish an 'Iberian Atlantic' Command with headquarters in Portugal. This meant moving from Norfolk, not from Paris. The *Richmond Times-Dispatch* hailed the establishment of I B E R L A N T (as the command is called) as a healthy sign of improved American relations with Portugal.

The Azores

In 1968 Vice-Admiral L. C. Heinz reported to the House of Representatives that 'our modest military assistance has helped to foster close working relationships with the Portuguese military'. The justification for this close working relationship, and one of the examples of it, is the continued American use of the base facilities in the Azores.

The Azores, principal reason for Portugal's admission to NATO originally, were important at the end of the Second World War and subsequently as a stop-over point for Europe and the Middle East. Now, according to an article inserted in the *Congressional Record* by Senator Pell of Rhode Island (5 June 1969), 'the basic mission of the USAF in the Azores ... is to maintain Lajes (Field) as a bastion of defence in case of global war. The mission also calls for the United States to assist Portugal in local defence, to maintain a Navy air-sea rescue operation and a centre of operations for antisubmarine warfare and to run a weather station operation. The Military Airlift Command also uses Lajes as a shuttle point for mail, supplies, and personnel to our forces in Europe.'

The original purpose of the base has thus become of secondary importance. Although in 1962 some eighty per cent of US military air traffic depended on the Azores, by 1968 the percentage had dropped to twenty. James Reston, in his column of 5 March 1969, noted that Washington 'needs the Azores no longer, but the old arrangements go on'. For the Pentagon, of course, all bases are important: it is always possible to find a new use for one. David Abshire, writing for the Navy-connected Center for Strategic and International Studies at Georgetown University, points out two of the most important new uses for the Azores. The first would be as a shuttle point for airlifting troops to the Middle East, should refuelling rights be denied to American planes in Western Europe and North Africa. The other is an increasing emphasis on surveillance of the Soviet submarine fleet; since use of the Azores can cut flying time for the anti-submarine planes by several hours.

The *Congressional Record* article ventures into more general reflection on the strategic importance of the Azores. The author of the article, after visiting military personnel on the Azores, reflects that

the Pentagon does not make mistakes all the time. Undoubtedly it is looking forward to the day when the war in South Vietnam ends.

After that, our top brass knows the action will shift. . . . the Communists will try to take over completely the new African countries. . . . Red targets will include the overseas province of Angola in Portuguese West Africa and Mozambique in Portuguese East Africa. . . . And so this African area could well turn into another South Vietnam.

The Azores base provides $6 million a year in employment and purchases for the Portuguese economy. It is, admits the article in the *Congressional Record*, 'a highly overstaffed operation that is costing the American taxpayers a lot of money'. But, the article continued, 'it is a necessary operation when you take a logical and long range view of Portuguese-American relations'. That logical and long-range view obviously does not include the prospect of independence for Portugal's African colonies.

Covert and Indirect Military Support

Bilateral aid, N A T O cooperation, and the Azores bases represent official, public American involvement with the Portuguese military, although the attempt is made to deny the link with Africa. Other channels exist as well. One is 'ordinary' business ties. Another is the Central Intelligence Agency.

A modern army needs not only specifically military equipment, but a wide variety of transport. And for that it needs vehicles, tyres, and fuel. American and Western European companies are eager to supply what is needed, as is shown by some of the advertisements in Portuguese military journals. Advertisements for Jeeps, 'the all-terrain vehicle preferred by the armed forces', compete with Land-Rover and Mercedes-Benz. M A B O R, associated with the General Tire and Rubber Company of Ohio, boasts that it 'is present on the wheels of all vehicles, contributing to the renovation and maintenance of the equipment of our Armed Forces'. Mobil Oil claims that 'it has participated with pride in the struggle for the defence of the province'. Even Canadair, a subsidiary of General Dynamics, tried to get into the act with an advertisement for an amphibious vehicle 'with complete mobility in deep snow' (that one didn't sell).

The support of American business is important for the Portuguese war machine. (This is discussed further in Chapter Six.) That is just 'business as usual'. C I A involvement is not as open (the Agency does not advertise), and it was only by chance that, in 1965, C I A complicity in a plot to smuggle B-26 bombers to Portugal was revealed. Seven bombers had already been shuttled to Portugal from Tucson, Arizona, when U S customs, evidently not privy to the plan, caught up with the smugglers. The pilot, John Hawke, an R A F veteran, and a French count, Henri de Montmarin, were brought to court in Buffalo, New York, to stand trial for munitions smuggling. Their defence was that they had been hired by the C I A.

The story that emerged from the trial seemed to confirm their account. The deal was set up originally by the owner of Aero Associates, Inc., of Tucson, a man named Gregory Board. Board, in conversation with Portuguese government officials, had arranged to deliver ten B-26 bombers (the order was later increased to twenty). The Douglas B-26 bombers have been used, since the Second World War, for counter-insurgency operations in Vietnam, Laos, the Bay of Pigs, and the Congo. C I A involvement in these operations is well-known.

At the trial Lawrence Houston, the C I A General Counsel, testified that the C I A knew about the shipments at least five days before they began. Even so, he denied that the C I A had any involvement in the affair. Judge John Henderson informed attorneys that 'any question calculated to improperly discredit the United States and its representatives will be disallowed', and questioning along these lines was cut off.

Between June and September 1965, seven bombers were taken to Portugal. They went from Tucson to Rochester, New York; then to Newfoundland, the Azores; and finally to Tancos Air Base in Portugal. Hawke was questioned several times, by F B I, F A A, and Canadian Customs officials; but in each case reference to the code word 'Operation Sparrow' shortly produced a go-ahead. Even when, on his second flight, he buzzed the White House by mistake (in a bomber), he was allowed to continue – and no charges were brought.

Contact between Board and Hawke was made originally by

Martin Caidin, a writer on aeronautics and space, twelve of whose books are used by the US Military. Several, such as a book on the Hercules transport plane, have been produced in special editions for USIS distribution overseas. At the trial, he testified that in September he warned the CIA that 'somebody's going to blow the lid on this'. Evidently rivalries within the intelligence community finally brought the case to the surface. In the autumn of 1965, the United States testified at the United Nations that the smuggling had been a purely private affair which the government had stopped.

Articles detailing the CIA involvement appeared, however, in the *Saturday Evening Post* and in *Ramparts*. Hawke and de Montmarin were acquitted. Martin Caidin, in a letter to *Ramparts* (February 1967), tried to excuse his own involvement by claiming that there was massive Chinese involvement on the side of the Angolan rebels. He admitted, however, that *Ramparts*' 'reporting of the government involvement [was] uncannily accurate'. The United States did not demand the return of the bombers from Portugal.

'Good Working Relationships'

One final indicator of the good working relationships between Portuguese and American military men is the frequent visits back and forth, many of which are reported in the Portuguese press. Once or twice each year, the American military attachés in Lisbon make a tour of one or more of the 'overseas provinces', to observe and advise. In March 1962, USAF Commander-in-Chief Curtis LeMay was in Portugal visiting the bases of the Portuguese Air Force. In December of the same year the Portuguese Minister of the Navy visited naval installations in the United States, and received the 'Legion of Merit'. In 1963, seven high-ranking officers of the US Industrial College of the Armed Forces visited Portuguese industrial enterprises; 34 US officers were hosted on an official study tour of Angola; and Rear Admiral J. A. Tyree, Jr, visited Mozambique with units from the US Fleet of the South Atlantic.

More recently, General Kaulza de Arriaga, before being transferred from Portugal to command the military region of Mozambique in mid-1969, made a two-week visit to the United States, at State Department invitation. His talks with Vietnam veteran General Westmoreland and Air Force General Ryan were followed by a tour of military installations around the country. General de Arriaga has launched a new forward attack policy, intended to seize and hold the terrain occupied by FRELIMO forces.

Since the closure of the Suez Canal, American military strategists have given renewed emphasis to the route around the Cape, and thus the whole of Southern Africa. In contingency plans relating to the Indian Ocean, or to much of the oil from the Middle East, Southern Africa has taken on an increased importance. Already American warships en route to the Persian Gulf, hindered from stopping in South Africa by the publicity concerning *apartheid*, make regular stops in Luanda and Lourenço Marques. One more 'business-as-usual' contact solidifies American military cooperation with Portugal.

6 The Growing Stake of American Business in Portuguese Africa

Portugal's Economy and Finances

In the period of Portuguese history preceding Salazar's dictatorship, financial instability was persistent. Enormous sums were owed to Germany, to Britain, to France. In 1898, Britain and Germany even signed a secret treaty to split up the Portuguese colonies in compensation for the debts, should Portugal not be able to maintain control. The final straw was an incredible forgery in which an impostor succeeded in placing an order with the English company that printed Portugal's banknotes. The resultant inflation and scandal contributed to the military takeover which installed Salazar, first as Minister of Finance, then as Prime Minister. Salazar had been trained in accounting, and gave priority above all to a balanced budget and fiscal responsibility.

It is understandable, then, that the Salazar regime, although firmly committed to private enterprise, remained sceptical about foreign financial entanglements. Restrictions on foreign investment, and a reluctance to incur foreign debts, have been strong currents in Portuguese policy, countered only recently by the strong drive for foreign capital to finance development and the colonial wars.

Recent development plans have included major inputs of external financing. While the First Six-Year Plan (1953–8) included a comparatively small percentage of external financing, the Second Plan (1959–64) envisaged a contribution of 25 per cent from foreign sources. The Third National Development Plan (1968–73), in its original provisions for the overseas territories, expected 36 per cent of the investment total to come from non-Portuguese sources. The annual programmes for 1968 and 1969 involve 33 per cent and 40 per cent external financing respectively.

American participation, which accounted for all the external financing in the First Plan, has remained larger than that of any other country. The Export-Import Bank provided, between 1962 and 1968, $73,300,000 in loans to Portugal. One of the projects financed was the Tagus River bridge, built by a consortium of American firms headed by U S Steel and Morrison-Knudsen. Other Export-Import Bank loans, including one in 1970 for $18 million, have gone on the purchasing of aircraft for the Portuguese airlines T A P. Substantial financing has also come from private American sources, arranged generally through Dillon, Read & Co., investment bankers for South Africa, and many other foreign governments (Douglas Dillon was Secretary of the Treasury under President Kennedy). These include loans issued in 1962 ($20 million), 1963 ($35 million), 1964 ($20 million), 1965 ($20 million), 1966 ($20 million), and 1967 ($12 million). United Nations reports have not yet mentioned loans for 1968 and 1969.

The American banking community has also become more directly involved in Portuguese Africa. One of the principal banks in Angola and Mozambique is a joint venture of the Portuguese Totta-Aliança and Standard Bank of South Africa. Standard Bank operates in many former British territories in Africa, and the Chase Manhattan Bank, one of the banks involved in a consortium loan to the South African government, has bought a significant interest in the chain.

Portugal is also tied to the United States by trade. Although the United States plays a lesser role in Portugal's trade than does Western Europe, it is still an important customer and supplier. Portugal's principal exports are textiles, wood, wines, cork, and fish. Outside the protected market of the Portuguese colonies, Britain ranks as the most important customer, followed by the United States. Portugal's imports include raw materials (largely from the African colonies) and manufactured goods.

West Germany is the major supplier, followed by Britain, France, and, in fourth place, the United States.

It is difficult to estimate the amount of American private investment in Portugal. Western Europe, Japan, and South Africa are also involved, and Portugal's own giant Companhia União Fabril has holdings in many sectors of the economy. Subsidiaries of many large firms (Abbott Laboratories, Colgate-Palmolive, Eastman Kodak, Firestone, Ford, General Electric, General Motors, International Business Machines, etc.) are located in Portugal, but their role in the economy seems at present more in the distribution of imports than in production. Portugal's economy is dependent on 'external impulsion', according to the OECD Survey, but the main attraction for foreign investors seems to be the extraction of natural resources from Africa, rather than the development of industry in Portugal.

As we saw in Chapter One, even before the 1960s much of the economy of Portuguese Africa was foreign controlled. But the American role was, until recently, comparatively minor, consisting mainly of the oil exploration contracts signed by Esso and Gulf Oil. The major expansion of American business involvement has come after the beginning of the struggle for liberation in Angola and Mozambique, at the same time that the United Nations was passing resolution after resolution to condemn Portuguese colonialism and those who support it.

Interest has been stimulated particularly by the prospect of increased mineral production, the economic expansion associated with it, and, since 1965, by the new investment regulations. Prior to 1965, Portuguese government regulations generally required Portuguese participation in the capital and administration of enterprises established with foreign capital. Decree-law 46,312 of April 1965 makes it possible for enterprises without the participation of Portuguese capital to operate in Portugal and the 'overseas provinces'. More and more companies are taking advantage of the new opportunities.

Oil and Other Mineral Resources

American capital has played its most important role in the mining sector, and in petroleum prospecting and production in particular. Even in Guinea, which has very little non-Portuguese capital, an American company is searching for oil. Esso Guiné Exploration, Inc., a subsidiary of Standard Oil of New Jersey, has held exploration rights since 1958. And the latest contract was signed in 1967.

This contract specifies that the majority of the directors of the subsidiary company shall be Portuguese; that 20 per cent of the shares shall be allocated to the Portuguese government; and that the minimum initial capital shall be $1·5 million. In the first five years of the concession (1967–72), Esso promises to spend at least $10·6 million. The concession itself runs for forty-five years, and covers all the territory of Guinea – offshore and onshore. After five years, the concession area will be reduced to 75 per cent (chosen by Esso); after ten years the area will be reduced still further, to 25 per cent.

The exploration has not yet uncovered oil deposits, and is only one of many ventures for Esso, the world's largest oil company. But the investment from this one contract represents 75 per cent of the total investment in the extractive industry for the 1968–73 development plan in Guinea; and 29 per cent of the total investment envisaged in that plan.

In Mozambique the involvement of the oil companies is also limited as yet to the exploratory stage, but there are a number of firms which have signed contracts. Gulf Oil Company has been engaged in limited prospecting in Mozambique since 1948, holding a concession jointly with the Pan American Oil Company since 1958. Investment from 1958 to 1967 amounted to $22 million; and under the terms of the renewed concession, almost $10 million from 1967 to 1970. No petroleum has been discovered, but large deposits of natural butane gas have been found near Beira. It has been reported that a pipeline may be constructed to supply the gas to the Transvaal, in South Africa.

In recent years, other American companies, large and small,

have entered the competition. Sunray, Skelly and Clark share a concession in southern Mozambique, and were committed to spending slightly more than $3 million in the three-year concession period from 1968 to 1970. These companies are all 'smaller' American companies, with comparatively little overseas involvement. Sunray is controlled by the Pew family of Philadelphia; Skelly by J. Paul Getty. Clark Oil and Refining Company has its headquarters in Milwaukee; its involvement in the Mozambique concession is one of its first overseas ventures.

Multimillionaires Howard Pew and Paul Getty got their concession in October 1967. H. L. Hunt, of Texas, was not far behind. In December of the same year a concession was granted to Hunt International Petroleum, which agreed to spend a minimum of $2 million over a three-year period. Hunt and Pew are both well-known backers of right-wing causes, from Goldwater to the Life Line radio programmes.

In 1968 Texaco entered the picture with a concession offshore from the northernmost province of Cabo Delgado. The contract followed the usual pattern, with Texaco agreeing to spend a little less than $2 million during the initial three-year period. Altogether, then, four concessions have been granted to a total of seven American oil companies; and a total of almost $40 million in investment was pledged to the end of 1970. This represents the overwhelming majority of investment in oil exploration in Mozambique. The only other concession is to a consortium involving French, German, and South African capital, with pledged investment of slightly more than $4 million.

It is only in Angola, however, that the oil companies have been successful in their search. Petrangol and Angol, two companies involving Belgian, French and South African interests, are engaged in petroleum production and in a refinery near Luanda. But even more successful has been Gulf Oil Company, which began its exploration in Angola in 1957, and struck oil in 1966, in Cabinda, the enclave of Angola north of the Congo River. Gulf is the sole concessionaire in Cabinda, and thus the principal beneficiary of oil resources which will put Angola among the top oil-producing countries in Africa, and make Portugal self-sufficient in petroleum supplies. Gulf's expenditure on exploration and development to the end of 1969 was estimated at $130 million. Some $76 million for the present programme of expansion was expected to bring production up to 150,000 barrels a day in 1970.

Annual oil production in Angola from 1965 to 1968 averaged approximately 650 thousand tons (from the Angol and Petrangol production). With the addition of Cabinda, production for 1969 was estimated at 1·5 million tons; 7·5 million tons were expected in 1970; and, by 1973, a possible annual production of 15 million tons is predicted.

The profit to the Portuguese government from this production is substantial, given the size of Angola's economy. Payments include surface rents, bonuses, income tax, royalties, and concession payments, making it difficult to estimate the exact amount that Portugal receives. According to Gulf Oil itself, in a statement defending its involvement against criticism, the company paid to the Angolan Government, in 1969, $11 million – an amount equal to almost half the size of what Gulf cited as the Angolan defence budget in 1970. In 1970, Gulf noted, 'we expect to pay in about $5 million ... and this will gradually increase as production reaches its peak and levels out.'

Gulf's cooperation with the Portuguese is not limited to the financial arrangements. Part of the contract states that Portugal has the first option on the oil produced, if military or political needs so dictate. At present the Cabinda oil is being exported, with the supplies for the Luanda refinery coming from the Petrangol-Angol production. The importance of the Cabinda reserves is indicated, however, by Rebocho Vaz, former Governor-General of Angola:

As you know, oil and its derivatives are strategic materials indispensable to the development of any territory; they are the nerve-centre of progress, and to possess them on an industrial scale is to ensure essential supplies and to dispose of an important source of foreign exchange.

Apart from this, in the mechanized wars of our times, its principle derivative – petrol – plays such a preponderant part that without reserves of this fuel it is not possible to give the Army sufficient means and elasticity of movement. The machine is the infrastructure of modern war, and machines cannot move without fuel. Hence the valuable support of Angolan oils for our armed forces.

(*African World Annual*, 1967–8, p. 29)

Gulf's arrangement with the Portuguese also includes provisions for cooperation in defence of the area in which the oil is produced. The government agrees to take 'such measures as may be necessary to prevent third parties from interfering with the company's free exercise of its contractual rights'. In return, Gulf, along with other companies considered 'indispensable to the normal life of the territory', is required to help provide for its own defence, with its activities fitted into the government's civil defence structure.

The course of the armed struggle in Cabinda illustrates this cooperation. According to A. J. Venter, a South African journalist favourable to the Portuguese, in 1961 'the insurgents were successful in occupying more than 90 per cent of the enclave. . . . They were successful in routing the ill prepared Portuguese militia and police and stopped just short of the capital, Cabinda' (A. J. Venter, *The Terror Fighters*). Gulf was forced to suspend operations at the height of the raids, but soon moved back in as the Portuguese re-established some control. Portuguese efforts in Cabinda were particularly intensive after the 1966 oil strike; in 1967 Cabinda received the largest allocation for rural regrouping projects (strategic hamlets). The major focus of fighting in Angola has shifted to the east, but guerrilla action continues to some extent in Cabinda. Gulf's contractual rights are protected by the military force that Portugal, with Gulf's help, is able to mobilize.

The Cabinda discovery, and continuing expansion of the Petrangol and Angol areas of production, has aroused the interest of several other companies. Texaco has become associated with the Petrangol-Angol group, and is apparently seeking a concession of its own as well. In 1969, applications were pending from Standard Oil, Union Carbide Petroleum, Diversa International (Dallas), Tenneco, and Mobil Oil, to list only the American companies.

The search for other mineral resources has stepped up as well, and American companies are represented among the prospectors. Prospecting rights for diamonds have been granted to Diversa Incorporated (Dallas), and to the West Angolan Diamond Company (73 per cent controlled by Diamond Distributors Inc., of New York). These concessions, together with those granted to several South African firms, are the first to be granted to any company other than the Angola Diamond Company, which previously held a monopoly position.

Tenneco Angola Ltd (a subsidiary of Tenneco Corporation) has been granted exploration rights for sulphur, gypsum and anhydrite. Discovery of rich sulphur deposits was reported in May 1969; and it is expected that Tenneco may spend as much as $75 million developing the sulphur. Plans are being considered to construct a pipeline to transport the liquefied sulphur to the coast. Tenneco, originally a pipeline company, is, after much diversification and expansion, thirty-ninth in *Fortune*'s list of American industrial corporations.

The exploitation of iron ore resources in Cassinga and elsewhere in Angola has been carried on principally by West German interests (see Chapter Seven). American participation in this project has been limited so far to credits from the Export-Import Bank and General Electric for the purchase of locomotives (from General Electric) to transport the extracted ore.

Of the mineral production in Mozambique, columbo-tantalite is of particular importance to the United States. Columbo-tantalite is used in the manufacture of tough steels, and is classified as a strategic metal. Mozambique is one of the major world producers of columbo-tantalite, and exports its production to the United States and Britain.

American Supplies for the Portuguese Army

Cooperation of American business with Portugal is evident in production for the war effort, as well as in the exploitation of mineral resources. Judging by advertisements in the Portuguese military journals, and by statistics on investment and trade, this cooperation is concentrated particularly in the sector of transport. Earth-moving equipment ranks next only to equipment for iron and steel manufacture in American exports to Angola. Caterpillar Tractor Company operates a distribution outlet in Luanda, and is a major supplier of agricultural and other heavy equipment. Other companies are involved in the supply of oil, vehicles, and tyres.

Mobil Oil Corporation, although not involved in exploration for oil in Angola or Mozambique, has been and still is one of the major distributors of oil in Portugal, in Angola, and in Mozambique. In 1969 it was completing the construction of a plant in Luanda for oil storage and the processing of lubricating oil. As we have seen (p. 110), Mobil is quite frank about its contribution to the Portuguese war effort.

Oil is important to an army, but so are tyres for military vehicles. Engaged in satisfying this need is MABOR, a Portuguese company associated with General Tire and Rubber Company, of Akron, Ohio. MABOR's tyre factory at Luanda in 1967 accounted for 19 per cent of all new industrial capital in Angola. The factory went into production in 1968, and has been granted a monopoly for ten years. It is understandable, then, that MABOR should also proudly express itself in the pages of the *Jornal do Exército*.

In the supply of vehicles themselves, the United States faces competition particularly from West Germany's Mercedes-Benz (which supplies NATO model troop transports) and from Britain's Land-Rover. But Kaiser Jeep Company (now merged in a complicated deal with American Motors) has managed to get some orders from the Portuguese, sending the jeeps at first from the United States and then from its production facilities in South Africa. The United States government maintains that this does not violate the principle against the use of American weapons in Portuguese Africa: jeeps do not count as military unless they already have guns mounted on them.

Agricultural Exports to the United States

Although mining is of considerable importance to the Angolan economy, export of primary agricultural products remains the most important sector, accounting for some 60 per cent in value of total exports. The predominance of agriculture in Mozambique is even greater, as mineral exploration there is only in initial stages. Direct American investment in the agricultural sector is minimal, but in the area of trade the United States is of crucial importance to both Angola and Mozambique.

In the postwar period, coffee has become Angola's most important export, accounting for approximately 50 per cent in value of exports during recent years. It is produced primarily on European plantations in northern Angola, with some production coming from African peasants on much smaller farms. Angola's *Robusta* coffee, cheaper than *Arabica* and used especially for instant coffee, has fared comparatively well in the world market. Angola ranks fourth in coffee exports in the world, with 5·0 per cent of the world total in 1968 (Brazil ranked first with 38·0 per cent; then Colombia, with 12·7 per cent; and the Ivory Coast, with 5·6 per cent).

The major importers of coffee are the United States and Europe, each buying approximately 45 per cent of the coffee sold on the world market. Of Angola's production, almost 50 per cent goes to the United States, with the Netherlands, Portugal, and South Africa as other major customers. This export of coffee from Angola to the United States is therefore of central importance to Angola's economy, constituting about one-fourth of the total exports. Even in terms of the large American market, it also ranks as important. Angola supplies 7 per cent of the coffee in the United States, ranking as the third supplier behind Brazil and Colombia.

The coffee bought by the consumer in the United States is

normally a blend, with different proportions of coffee from various sources. The cup of coffee that the consumer drinks is therefore the product of a system that involves pressure on prices by the rich, coffee-consuming countries; erratic income to the coffee-producing countries; and the exploitation of workers in both Latin America and in Angola. The coffee that comes from the plantations of northern Angola is now often transported by military vehicles, and with the protection of armed guards. The plantations, too, are armed camps, for the coffee-growing country in Angola has been the scene of guerrilla warfare since the initial insurrection in 1961. Business continues as usual, however, for the coffee exporters in Luanda, and the coffee importers in New York.

The United States is not a major customer for other agricultural exports of Angola. Nor is it for most of the products of Mozambique. But cashew nuts, of which Mozambique produces approximately half the world's exports – India and Tanzania are the other major producers – find their primary eventual destination in the US market. Until recently, most of the nuts were sent unshelled to India for the complicated processing necessary to remove the poison contained in the shell. The introduction of processing equipment into Mozambique (with the help of Italian, British, and South African capital) is expected to increase the percentage of shelled nuts in the exports. The United States buys about 90 per cent of the processed products, including the nuts and cashew nut shell liquor, which has many industrial uses and is classified as of strategic importance.

The Significance of American Economic Involvement

In proportion to the full range of American economic involvement overseas, the ties with Portuguese Africa still seem rather minor. For this reason, the argument is often raised that such ties are not really important in determining American policy towards the area. Such an argument, however, rests on a basic fallacy: for the relevant comparison is with other possible influences on American policy, and not with the mere fact of involvements elsewhere. Any conflict with American interests elsewhere in Africa is ignored, or minimized. Gulf's operations in Angola have not prevented the company from getting involved elsewhere in Africa. Only if other African states forced American business and government to make a choice would involvement both in white-controlled Africa and black Africa become a real contradiction. In the actual context, increased involvement in Portuguese Africa, which includes some of the largest American corporations and influential financial institutions, provides powerful reinforcement to the military, strategic, and other 'Cold War' influences already at work. A focus on development in Africa by the cooperation of Portugal and foreign interests becomes one more assumption shared by those dealing with American foreign policy.

A striking example of the propagation of such ideas has been the Hudson Institute's 'flying think tank' visit to Angola in September 1969, and the subsequent report. Hudson, the brainchild of former Rand Corporation staffer and futurologist Herman Kahn, is one of the influential research institutes financed largely by Defense Department contracts. Such studies as 'Can We Win in Vietnam?' (the answer was yes) and a recent book defending the ABM are two products of the Hudson Institute. The Institute has become involved as well in 'poverty' and 'development' projects, and is notorious in Brazil for its proposal to create a series of 'Great Lakes' in the interior of Latin America. Its members include scholars, corporation executives, and people particularly concerned with foreign affairs, such as Frank Altschul, the Vice-President of the Council on Foreign Relations.

The visit to Angola, and a subsequent conference in Estoril, Portugal, were sponsored by the Companhia União Fabril, the largest company in Portugal. The report contains comments and suggestions by team members and other Hudson Institute staff on the prospects for development in Angola.

Hopping over the countryside in small planes, they saw few signs of war, and emerged with optimistic predictions on the Portuguese ability to control insurgency. The attitude to insurgency itself was revealed by Herman Kahn's proposals after receiving the team report. He suggested the use of computers to keep track of every person, and noted:

> This proposal has been turned down by the United States because it looks too authoritarian.... It could be done in Portugal, and a paternalistic country might well want to keep interested in every single individual. This can be put in for health purposes, for education purposes, for advancement purposes.... It is a tremendous research tool.... It is a tool which can be abused. But again, thinking of Angolan insurgency, it probably is the best police instrument known to mankind, which is both its plus and its minus. The plus is that it means one can keep down violence without being nasty; can be efficient and quick rather than nasty and hard. The minus is that if one wants to sit rather than change (as in the book 1984) it gives one a chance for that.
>
> (*Hudson Institute Report HI-1278-/RR1*, p. 29)

The Hudson team has produced three possible scenarios for the development of Angola: business as usual; 'cut-and-run development'; or 'go for broke', rapid, large-scale development. Business as usual means simply staying with present development programmes. The second choice means to 'concentrate on industries which by their nature can be removed in case of trouble or cannot be operated by unskilled native labour'. The final possibility, most favoured by Hudson, assumes that the Portuguese military will retain control, and that 'premature withdrawal is irresponsible as it is a way of turning people over to control by small cliques'. The idea then presented is to consider massive development projects, like damming the Congo River (a project that 'could be the first real bridge between a black African state and a European province'), large-scale oil refining, or large-scale cattle ranching. All such schemes would, of course, involve substantial inputs of external capital.

Hudson's grandiose 'think tank' ideas may be particularly extravagant and removed from reality (even many of its studies for the office of Civil Defense were judged superficial and worthless by that office). But the assumptions on which these are based are important. For those assumptions – of a continued Portuguese presence, and of the consequent opportunities for American investment – are shared by a substantial majority of those who deal at high levels with American foreign policy, be they business men, government officials, or the establishment's foreign policy academics.

7 Portugal's Other Allies: The 'Free World' Defends Colonialism

The United States has seen itself, in the years following the Second World War, as leading a bloc of countries known as the 'Free World'. The support which Portugal receives from this wider grouping headed by the United States is perhaps even more important today than the direct bilateral American support. Among NATO's other members, Great Britain, West Germany, and France are particularly important to Portugal. South Africa's economic and military strength sustains the Portuguese in Angola and Mozambique, and is supported in turn by other Western powers. Brazil, a potential ally for African liberation in Portuguese Africa, ties itself instead more closely to Portugal, and even to South Africa. Thus the middle-level countries of the American hegemony take their places, also, on the side of Portugal.

South Africa: Keystone of White Rule in Southern Africa

Of all the countries on which Portugal depends for help in sustaining her colonial rule in Africa, the Republic of South Africa is certainly of the most direct importance. And, in spite of their supposedly opposite views on race relations, and the territorial competition of the late nineteenth century, the two white powers have for some time recognized their interdependence. Caetano, on his visit to Africa as Minister of Colonies in 1945, received Field-Marshal Smuts of South Africa at a banquet in Lourenço Marques, and spoke of the 'many common problems which concern us in the great drama of the adaptation of Europeans to African soil'. Mozambique's role in providing labour for South

Africa, and transport links for its commerce, has also been noted in Chapter One.

But of late, the incentive for close cooperation has been more immediate, and is inducing a new push towards closer ties, both military and economic. The South African Foreign Minister, speaking in April 1969, put the common understanding quite clearly:

> We are two very friendly countries and we are perfectly identified with each other as defenders of civilization in Africa. We have a common mission to fulfil and we are fulfilling it. We South Africans, government and people, respect and admire Portugal, and we are fully aware that, in confronting and defeating terrorism, the Portuguese are rendering a noteworthy service to the West and to humanity itself.

This common understanding has resulted in common military planning, despite the absence of a public treaty of military co-operation. Portuguese, South African, and Rhodesian military and police officials hold periodic high-level consultations, and are in touch with each other as well on a day-to-day basis. South African troops and helicopters have been reported in action in southern Angola. In Tete province of Mozambique, the Cabora Bassa area is also under South African guard. The South African advance air bases in Caprivi and the northern Transvaal are ideally sited to cover areas of Angola and Mozambique as well.

Nevertheless South Africa has not yet become as heavily involved in Angola and Mozambique as it is in Rhodesia, where South African 'police' form a major portion of the counterinsurgency forces. How much South African involvement grows depends on how well Portugal itself is able to maintain the *status quo*. There is feeling already among some white South Africans that not enough is being done to help Portugal; and projects such as the Mozambique Soldiers' Comfort Fund have sprung up in South Africa, to help those who are seen as being on the front lines for the whites of South Africa. Indeed, South Africa would be very likely to intervene on a large scale to prevent southern

Mozambique from coming under hostile control. Heavy involvement in Angola or northern Mozambique would be more difficult, risking an over-extension of South Africa's defence perimeter. But even this cannot be ruled out, especially if it appeared that these areas would come under the control of radical rather than collaborationist African leaders.

But the military ties do not exhaust the network of cooperation in Southern Africa. Just as significant is the role that Angola and Mozambique play in South Africa's plans for an integrated bloc in Southern Africa, and perhaps extending even further north. In these plans the hydroelectric projects on the Zambezi and Cunene Rivers are of central importance.

In Angola the Matala Salazar powerplant on the Cunene River, in the extreme south, has been the source of power for southern Angola. Its power and irrigation capacity is to be expanded, and the entire area developed in a joint project with South Africa. Power will be provided not only for Angola, but also for South-West Africa. Portuguese plans call for settlement of large numbers of immigrants in the area opened up. When completed, the Cunene Basin river scheme will represent the largest South African investment in Angola.

Of even more significance is the Cabora Bassa hydroelectric project, in Tete province, Mozambique. The project is to be developed in four stages, the first of which is to be completed by 1974. The power output is scheduled to be double that of Kariba, or 70 per cent more than Aswan, and will feed into a power network serving all of Southern Africa, particularly South Africa and Rhodesia.

The scheme has been developed in close cooperation with the Industrial Development Corporation of South Africa, and the contract for construction was granted eventually to a consortium headed by the Anglo-American Corporation of South Africa, with participation as well by German and French firms. A Swedish and an Italian firm initially involved have withdrawn, and work has now begun under the leadership of Anglo-American. The importance of the Cabora Bassa scheme is illustrated by the South African troops there, and by FRELIMO attacks in the immediate vicinity. At present, African populations in the area are being moved out and regrouped in strategic hamlets, both to make way for the dam, and to counter FRELIMO influence among the people.

South African involvement is also present and growing in many sectors of the economies of Angola and Mozambique. A summary picture can be gained by looking at the involvement of one financial group, Harry Oppenheimer's Anglo-American Corporation. In Angola the Benguela Railway, which provides an access to the seas for the copper of Zambia and Katanga, is 90 per cent owned by Tanganyika Concessions, Ltd. Among the larger shareholders in Tanganyika Concessions is Anglo-American Corporation; British and Belgian capital is also involved. DIAMANG, the Angola Diamond Company, provides approximately 5 per cent of the revenue of the government of Angola, and runs a virtual 'state within a state' in the diamond producing area. Anglo-American Corporation, together with Belgian and American interests, controls it as well. Anglo-American is also involved directly or indirectly in other mineral prospecting in Angola.

In Mozambique Anglo-American Corporation's ties are less concentrated in already established operations, but spread into almost every developing sector of the economy. Its role in the Cabora Bassa consortium has already been mentioned. It is also involved in one of the oil exploration concessions (jointly with a German and a French firm). It is involved in diamond prospecting, and in prospecting for other minerals in Tete province. It has gained a stake in sugar production near Quelimane; is developing a cashew factory near João Belo; and controls Mozambique's only substantial fishing enterprise. The traditional labour export and communications provided by Mozambique serve the Rand mines area, where Anglo-American is one of the major enterprises. It would be difficult to find a sector of Mozambique's economy in which Anglo-American does not play an important role. Even in Portugal, Anglo-American is now the owner of one of the largest wolfram mines.

Recent reports refer to South African and Portuguese talks on nuclear energy activities. Links of all kinds continue to grow. The challenge to Portuguese colonial rule is faced by the spectre of greater South African intervention to come.

Great Britain: The Ancient Alliance Continued

If the ties with South Africa are of most immediate importance to Portugal, those with Great Britain are of the longest duration. The Anglo-Portuguese Alliance dates from 1373, and, with many ups and downs, has survived through all the subsequent changes in the European political scene. It was Great Britain that set the limits to Portugal's acquisition of African territory, and that assumed the dominant investment role in Angola and Mozambique. It was also British humanitarians who raised the hue and cry about the continued slave trade to São Tomé, and through a boycott forced such reforms as were made.

The economic interests of Britain in Portugal and her colonies are of long standing. A British company runs the public transport of Lisbon. Britain plays the major foreign role in the port wine trade. The largest Portuguese producer of wolfram, Beralt Tin and Wolfram Company, was British-owned until 1968 (now South African capital also is involved). There are seven British factories assembling motor vehicles in Portugal. In all, British investments in 1968 represented 25 per cent of all foreign investments in Portugal.

In Africa the role of the Anglo-American Corporation has already been discussed. Although primarily South African based, Anglo-American involves substantial British capital. In Angola the British Oxygen Company and the British-owned Sociedade Agrícola do Cassequel are both substantial investors. In Mozambique British capital, through Sena Sugar Estates and Spence and Pierce, Lda, plays the major role in the production of sugar.

Great Britain is also still Portugal's most important trading partner; in 1968 she was ranked first in imports from Portugal (nearly twice the second-ranking U S A), and second only to West Germany in exports to Portugal. With the colonies also, Great Britain has retained an important role as a trading partner, although the decision to introduce diamond cutting in Portugal has sharply reduced exports from Angola to London. In spite of the competition from West Germany and the United States, Britain's joint membership with Portugal in the European Free Trade Association provides continuing advantages for British interests.

Britain's traditional influence over Portugal is illustrated by the negotiations leading to the use of the Azores bases in the closing years of the Second World War. It is also, surprisingly, reflected in the recent Rhodesian crisis. Although Portugal has been active in helping Rhodesia to avoid sanctions, and is engaged in constant military and economic cooperation with Smith's regime, British pressure to keep up appearances resulted in the official withdrawal of the Portuguese Consul from Rhodesia in 1970.

What influence Britain has, however, has not been exerted against continuing Portuguese colonial rule. Its record in the United Nations has, since 1962, been consistently negative: voting against or abstaining on resolutions condemning Portuguese colonialism. And military cooperation under NATO auspices has continued on the same basis as that of the United States with Portugal.

In 1961, shortly after the beginning of the war in Angola, two frigates were sold by the British government to Portugal. Reassurances were given that they would be used only 'to meet Portugal's NATO obligations'. According to notices in Portugal's *Revista da Marinha*, both have served almost all their time since 1961 in waters off Angola or Mozambique. Between 1961 and 1964, Britain supplied to Portugal 150 light aircraft (Auster), for the use of the Air Force. And a sale of 300 Austin Jeeps to the Army was made in 1965. Land-Rover, too, is in the competition to supply vehicles to the Army.

The new Conservative government can be expected to maintain even closer relations with Portugal. Mr John Biggs-Davidson, a Conservative M.P., has taken it upon himself to be a constant spokesman for Portuguese interests, denying that there is any war in Africa, and emphasizing the strategic importance of the Portuguese territories for the West. Although the extreme suggestion of a South Atlantic Treaty Organization (pushed by South Africa and Portugal) may not get a favourable response, the importance of the sea route around the Cape is a theme that gets a sympathetic hearing among Conservatives. A government that promises to reopen arms sales to South Africa is hardly likely to put new restraints on arms to Portugal. The new government can also be expected to encourage the expansion of commercial ties prefigured by the Anglo-Portuguese Conference on Trade and Investments (November 1969), and by the recent visits of British businessmen to Portugal and Angola.

Help from the Federal Republic of Germany

The Anglo-Saxon powers feel it necessary to cover up their support for Portuguese colonialism with a veil of hypocrisy: talk of self-determination, and denial that their military aid has anything to do with Africa. West Germany, perhaps because it does not have to take stands in the United Nations, perhaps because it has no strong tradition of anti-colonial protest, seems to feel no such necessity. In the sixties West Germany has become one of Portugal's most important trading partners, with close diplomatic and military relations proceeding apace.

After the Second World War Portugal was the only country which did not confiscate the property of German nationals. At Hitler's death, flags in Lisbon were flown at half-mast. And Portugal eagerly joined the United States in pressing for the admission of the German Federal Republic to N A T O. This friendship has been symbolically reciprocated with numerous visits of West German dignitaries to Portugal. Dr Richard Jaeger, then Vice-President of the Bundestag and chairman of its defence commission, after a visit to Angola and Mozambique in 1963, expressed himself in these terms:

Only under the Salazar government ... is an upswing noticeable both in the mother country and in the overseas regions.... I feel that the word 'foreign rule' is not appropriate for territories under Portuguese administration for almost five hundred years, and that probably also the natives – at least in the biggest part of the country – do not consider it as such. . . . I consider it not only a moral but also a political principle to be loyal to one's friends. In the case of Portugal this has special reasons.

(*Rheimische Merkur,* August 1963)

West German loyalty has expressed itself in substantial military cooperation with Portugal. In 1963 an agreement was negotiated by which the West German Air Force would acquire use of an air base in Beja, Portugal, constructed with German aid. A German military mission, with a staff of about 100, was established in Lisbon to coordinate military relations between the two countries. Germany's contribution, in exchange for use of the air base, includes medical treatment in Germany for seriously wounded Portuguese soldiers; the supply of arms and aircraft; and, it seems, special training for Portuguese espionage units.

Portugal's Air Force, supplied during the 1950s primarily by the United States, has in recent years received much of its new equipment from Germany. In 1966 West Germany supplied forty Fiat G-91 fighter-bombers, particularly suited to counter-insurgency use. A *pro forma* statement by the German Defence Ministry stated that they were to be used within the NATO area, for defence purposes. Portugal quickly clarified that Portuguese territory included Angola, Mozambique, and Guinea. West German spokesmen do not bother to deny that the planes are being used in Africa.

More recently, over 100 Dornier DO-27s, a light counter-insurgency aircraft, have been supplied to Portugal. These are produced in West Germany, and, along with the American T-6s, form the backbone of Portugal's air power in Africa. A journalist visiting Mozambique in March 1970 observed the DO-27 in action, bombing villages in the FRELIMO-controlled areas of Cabo Delgado province.

The Blohm & Voss shipyard in Hamburg, West Germany, is constructing three warships of 1,400 tons each for Portugal. They are the largest constructed in Germany since the Second World War. According to the *Revista da Marinha,* the ships are especially equipped for 'intensive use in the Overseas

Provinces'. The first of the three to be completed has already been delivered to Portugal.

Germany also cooperates in the supply of small arms for Portugal's wars. In 1961, Germany arranged for the transfer to Portugal of 10,000 UZI guns from Israel. The G-3 NATO model gun is now produced in Portugal at a factory run jointly by the Germans and the Portuguese.

One further kind of military cooperation is difficult to document in detail, but cannot be dismissed. A London periodical (*Private Eye*, 9 May 1969) reported that in 1968 West German intelligence officers were made available to PIDE (the Portuguese secret police), and cooperated in the campaign against FRELIMO, which culminated in the assassination of President Eduardo Mondlane. The action coincided with the German entry into the Cabora Bassa hydroelectric project, and with FRELIMO's new offensive in Tete province.

The West German firm Siemens Aktiengesellschaft has an important role in the ZAMCO consortium responsible for the Cabora Bassa project. When first ASEA (Swedish) and then English Electric withdrew from part of the project, Siemens took over their role as well. Other German firms involved in the consortium are Telefunken; the German subsidiary of Brown, Boveri Ltd; Hochtief; and J. M. Voith Gmbh. Protests from FRELIMO, and from African states with which Germany has ties, proved ineffective.

German capital is involved as well in exploration for petroleum and coal in Mozambique. Of most importance, however, is the involvement of Krupp and other interests in exploiting the iron of Cassinga in southern Angola. The Companhia Mineira do Lobito, financed by Fried. Krupp (Essen), and to a lesser extent by other international interests (Jagjaard and Schulz, of Denmark; the US Export-Import Bank; and others), has in recent years rapidly increased iron ore production: from one million tons in 1967, to three million in 1968, and almost six million in 1969. The Moçamedes railway and harbour have been improved, and yet further expansion is expected. The major customers for the ore are Japan and Germany.

It might have been expected that the new German government, under Social Democrat Willy Brandt, would take a different line on Portuguese colonialism. After all, the social democratic parties in Sweden and Britain had exerted some pressure for withdrawal of firms in their countries from the ZAMCO consortium. And in any event, with Germany's drive for economic expansion in the rest of Africa, some sensitivity to opinion in black Africa might have been predicted. But no real evidence of a change in policy exists.

The Tanzanian party newspaper *The Nationalist* called attention to West German conduct in an editorial of 9 February 1970, and asked, 'Does this mean that West Germany, despite changes in its European policies, has finally and irrevocably chosen its side in the Southern African conflict? Surely it can mean little else.... Does Germany think we do not care? Or that we do not notice?'

France: Support without Scruples

France's involvement in Southern Africa, with both South Africa and Portugal, is idiosyncratic. France has no inhibitions about giving explicit military aid, and openly denies any United Nations jurisdiction in such situations. At the same time, French involvement tends to be specific and limited, and for some reason does not attract the same attention as the comparable support given by Germany or Britain. The reason may be that French overseas involvement is highly concentrated in former French-controlled areas; that none of these are located in Southern Africa; and that France has been able to attract Third World sympathy by attacking (on other grounds) *les anglo-saxons*. The fact remains that less attention is paid to French involvement, and there is consequently less information available about it. In Africa, most of the francophone countries are still heavily influenced by France, and reluctant to make such criticism. And the English-speaking countries seem to have followed their lead.

French military aid to Portugal, unlike that from other NATO countries, is supplied with no official restriction as to where it can be used. The most important single item supplied is the Alouette helicopter, produced by Sud-Aviation. Portugal has obtained both Alouette-2 and Alouette-3 models in substantial numbers. Other aircraft obtained from France include the transports Nord 2502 Noratlas, Holste Broussard, and Junker JU-52.

In 1967–9 four frigates and four submarines were received by Portugal, built in France and financed with a $100 million loan guaranteed by the French government. Panhard armoured cars were being used in Portugal at the beginning of the war in Angola; and Portugal has received new supplies of these cars, for use in Africa.

France has profited from the relationship with Portugal by obtaining a base of its own on the Azores, opened in 1965 as a tracking station for French missiles. During the Nigerian Civil War, Portugal also served as a conduit for French aid to Biafra. With the collapse of Biafra the possibility for extensive French influence there, and consequent control over the sources of petroleum, disappeared. It may well be that France will now pay increasing attention to the possible sources of oil and other minerals in Angola and Mozambique.

Indeed, the major focus of French economic involvement prior to the Cabora Bassa project has been oil. The Angol company, involved in oil production in Angola, is controlled by SACOR, the Portuguese refining and distributing company. SACOR in turn is reportedly controlled by the French state-owned Compagnie Française des Pétroles. SACOR's attitude is expressed concisely in an advertisement appearing in the *Jornal do Exército*: 'Sacor . . . at the service of the Portuguese Army'.

France is involved as well, through the Société Nationale des Pétroles Aquitaines, in exploration for oil in Mozambique. Other investments include sugar production (in Mozambique) and Alumínio Português (in Angola). Four French firms are involved in the ZAMCO consortium on the Cabora Bassa project. There are no reports as yet of substantial French involvement in the rush of mineral exploration in Tete province; but it would be surprising if such involvement did not occur soon.

France's general stance is clear. She has no scruples about co-operation with Portuguese colonialism. The theory backing Portuguese colonialism (that the colonies are an integral part of the nation) is familiar to the French from their own background. France ranks in fourth place among exporters to Portugal, and fifth as a buyer of Portuguese exports. There are more Portuguese immigrant workers in France than in any other country. France's UN votes on questions of colonialism are consistently negative. French policy is not likely to change. And French involvement, as supplier of military equipment and of capital investment, will continue, and probably grow.

Brazil: A New Afro-Asian Policy Reversed

Brazil has the largest population of any country in Latin America and the largest population of Portuguese-speakers in the world. Although used by the Portuguese as an example of 'assimilation', political independence from the mother country goes as far back as 1822. In the future of Portuguese-speaking Africa, it could be of great importance. Even now, if the Brazilian government were sympathetic, students from Angola and Mozambique could be sent to secondary schools and universities in Brazil. As it is, students sent overseas by the liberation movements must learn yet another non-African language, undertaking their studies in English, or French, or Russian. The possibilities for fruitful cooperation between Brazil and an independent Angola and Mozambique would be considerable.

But such ties with African nationalists do not now exist. The reason lies partly in Brazil's traditional ties of friendship with Portugal, but also in the story of a new foreign policy aborted by the American-backed coup of 1964. Brazil's incipient attempts to move into solidarity with the rest of the Third World, and to abandon automatic adherence to the Western bloc, were cut off, even more suddenly than were the first steps in Kennedy's anti-colonial image-building.

The ties that existed between Portugal and Brazil after Brazil's independence were less ones of economic interdependence than they were cultural and sentimental. Portuguese immigrants came to Brazil, but for the most part they were not the influential kind. Brazil has its 'Portuguese' jokes just as the United States has its jokes about Poles or other immigrants. The ties were close, and affirmed especially by those who made Brazil's foreign policy, but they could not be regarded as crucial for Brazil. Perhaps more important in the determination of post-Second World War policy towards Portugal was simply the tendency to follow without question the United States or the Western European powers on international issues, including votes in the UN on colonialism.

The first significant break with this general line came with the brief regime of Jânio Quadros, and this was continued by his successor, João Goulart. Relations were opened up with the countries of Eastern Europe, of Asia, and of Africa. Brazil voted in 1962 for General Assembly resolution 1742, which condemned Portugal for its actions in Angola. Scholarships were arranged for African students, and several visits by Brazilian dignitaries were arranged to independent African states. Articles and books appeared about the new 'independent' foreign policy. The study of Africa and Asia grew by leaps and bounds.

It is true that Brazil's policy towards Portuguese Africa was still marked by ambiguity, much as was that of the United States. The break with Portugal on voting did not extend to support of more serious action by the United Nations. But the ties with Portugal were under serious question; the automatic dependence on American policy was rejected; and there seemed to be a serious possibility of further changes. The vision of Brazil as a leading force in the Third World was a compelling one.

The military coup of 1964, followed within hours by congratulations from Washington, marked a reversal not only in Brazil's domestic policies, but also in the stance taken on the world scene. Brazil moved back, to a position of 'interdependence'; interdependence, that is, within the Western bloc. President Castello Branco, in his news conference of 30 October 1964, commented specifically on policy towards Portugal's overseas provinces:

Brazil, although reaffirming its position on the subject of self-determination, will emphasize its conviction that Portugal will know how to solve its problems in the spirit of its historic traditions, traditions that presided over the formation of the Brazilian national soul and gave form to the type of multiracial society that is dominant in Brazil. The confidence of Brazil in the civilizing mission of Portugal thus derives from the consideration of concrete facts, confirmed by sociology and history.

Addressing the United Nations in December 1964, the Brazilian Ambassador lauded peaceful decolonization, and condemned those who would inject violence in the process. It was the same line as that followed by the United States. The Ambassador talked of self-determination; but the example he gave was that of Germany and its reunification, not Africa. That same year, Brazil even voted against the General Assembly's resolution on sanctions against South Africa, maintaining that (in contrast to the Cuban case) the South African problem was purely an internal one.

The trend towards closer solidarity with Africa and Asia was reversed. Relations with mainland China were broken. Angolans studying in Brazil were harassed by the Portuguese secret police. African studies languished or concentrated almost exclusively on folklore. It is true that embassies were maintained in African countries, and possibilities for commercial ties continued to be explored. President Senghor of Senegal even visited Brazil after the coup. But the joint communiqué made no reference to the armed struggle against Portugal in Senegal's next-door neighbour Guinea-Bissau. And the next year Foreign Minister Nogueira of Portugal visited Brazil to discuss plans for closer Brazilian-Portuguese cooperation.

Now, South Africa and Portugal have joined forces to push closer cooperation in the South Atlantic. They are wooing Brazil and Argentina with the prospects of increased trade, tourism, and military consultation. Their dream is for a South Atlantic Treaty Organization, to protect the two sides of the southern ocean from the dangers of 'communist aggression'.

Portugal has continued to play on the theme of a Luso-Brazilian community. In 1967, a Brazilian naval squadron was sent on a training mission to Angola. The admiral in charge noted: 'we are deeply shocked that a war is being waged against Portugal in her overseas territories. ... We will do everything we can for Portugal which is the victim of a great injustice.' The naval visits continued, and 1969 saw the first visit in decades of a Portuguese Premier to Brazil. Caetano succeeded in obtaining pledges of commercial and cultural exchanges, and presumably the military visits will continue as well; but he failed to get any specific pledge of military cooperation.

Since 1965 Portugal's persuasive efforts have been joined by South African initiatives in Latin America. In 1965 South Africa participated in a Latin American Development Bank project in Ecuador, and followed in 1968 with purchases of bonds from the Bank. In 1966 a visit by the South African Minister of Foreign Affairs to Brazil, Argentina, Uruguay, and Paraguay prompted return trade missions and appearances by Brazil and Argentina at the Rand Easter Show in Johannesburg. In September 1966, a Portuguese–Brazilian agreement facilitated the transhipment of goods between South Africa and Brazil in ports of Portuguese Africa.

In 1969 joint exercises by the South African and Argentine navies, combined with a trip to Rio de Janeiro and Buenos Aires by the South African Foreign Minister, prompted renewed speculation about a South Atlantic Treaty Organization. It is rumoured that Argentina lost its seat on the UN Development Programme to Cuba because of the annoyance of the African bloc at these developments.

The South African Airways flight established between New York and Johannesburg passes through Rio de Janeiro. And Varig, the Brazilian airline, is now setting up flights to South Africa as well. Tourism will be further encouraged by the luxury liner *Queen Elizabeth II*, stopping in Luanda, Capetown, Buenos Aires, and Rio de Janeiro. Trade and investment ties are also likely to increase, although the Southern African and Latin American economies tend to be competitive rather than complementary. Some military ties, such as joint naval exercises, may well continue.

But Brazil and Argentina, however reactionary they may be, are still reluctant to enter into any open alliance with the explicit racism of South Africa, or to get heavily involved in Portugal's colonial wars. Their talk is much like that of the United States on the same issues. The context is the South Atlantic, but the policy is in accordance with the North American lead. Brazil's fling at an 'independent foreign policy' is temporarily over; and now solidarity in the South Atlantic is not for Third World liberation, but for repression.

Cooperative Support for Colonial Repression

The struggle for liberation from Portuguese colonial rule might be seen as dealing simply with an anachronism; with a country that refuses to face up to the realities of today's world. But to stop there in the analysis would be a dangerous illusion. For Portugal's colonialism, anachronistic as it is, can count on the support of the United States, which considers it a part of the 'Free World'. In this context it also gains support from other members of that bloc, and the fight against Portuguese colonialism must reckon with support for Portugal from France, Germany, Britain, South Africa, and even Brazil. The United States might wish to isolate the issue, so as to ignore it more easily; but the support given to Portugal internationalizes it instead.

8 What Future for American Policy?

The previous chapters have described American policy and the numerous forms of American support given to Portuguese colonial rule in Africa. The description of that policy, and of the forces behind it, imply in themselves some predictions about the future. To leave it at that, however, would be to give a false impression, that other policy options are not only unlikely but impossible. The pressure of events may finally compel some other response from those who make American policy, and it is important to consider what that response might be.

To answer such a question, it is necessary to ask first who is involved in the formation of foreign policy. The general public certainly is not. One of the most strongly substantiated conclusions from a study of foreign policy is the wide extent of public uninvolvement in even the most basic of issues. The average citizen may have strong opinions about the domestic issues that affect him most directly – jobs, schools, taxes, housing. But foreign policy is by and large distant and remote. To bring the public into the debate takes a major issue which has direct effects on people, and on which there is substantial dissent among those already involved in policy. Even Congress usually plays for the most part a minor, secondary role in the making of foreign policy. It is the executive branch of the government, the large corporations involved overseas, and such elite clusters as the Council on Foreign Relations that set the assumptions and make the policy.

Within this foreign policy elite there are strong forces favouring the *status quo* policy on Portuguese colonialism, and setting limits on the kind of change that can take place in the future, even if change is forced. As we have seen, two prominent sources of inertia are the military on the one hand, and an orientation to Europe on the other.

The interest of the military is clear. Portugal is an ally in America's most important military alliance. It is anti-communist, stable, and friendly. And Southern Africa is of growing importance, to counter the threat of the Soviet Navy in the Indian Ocean, and to maintain control of the route around the Cape. Many military men are clearly sympathetic to Portugal's views on her problems in Africa. And their ability to defend their position in Washington, particularly when they can appeal to national security (the Azores, European defence, the Soviet threat), is well known.

But they rarely have to defend their position on this issue. For the assumption generally prevails that European interests automatically take precedence over African, even when the European country involved is a small and relatively unimportant one such as Portugal. Europe, Asia, and Latin America are recognized as primary areas of American 'responsibility'; Africa is peripheral. George Ball spoke for many besides himself, when he suggested we 'recognize that Africa [is] a special European responsibility just as today the European nations recognize our particular responsibility in Latin America' (*The Discipline of Power*, p. 241). Clearly this does not mean that the United States has no interests in Africa. It is simply that the policy-makers wish to keep any open involvement 'low-profile'; to play down problems in the hopes that someone else will deal with them, or that they will go away.

The military and European emphases are joined in support of the *status quo* policy by the American understanding of what 'development' in Africa should mean. 'Stability' is important, and, after independence, the former colonial powers can be important stabilizing forces. So, according to the Department of State *Background Notes*, 'the United States recognizes the contribution made in Africa by Portugal and believes that it is important that Portugal continue to contribute to stability in that continent'. The United States would prefer that contribution to be provided with a façade of self-determination. But, as

G. Mennen Williams remarks in his book, ironically entitled *Africa for the Africans*, 'this does not necessarily mean that independence would be the end result' (p. 132).

Such a policy, which requires a peaceful transition to political self-determination in which Portuguese interests are safeguarded, is obviously at odds with the present realities of Portuguese intransigence and the protracted guerrilla warfare in Angola, Mozambique, and Guinea-Bissau. In the interim, the 'stability' is sufficient for Gulf and others to make their plans and extract their profits. As long as guerrilla victory does not appear imminent, the contradiction can be easily tolerated by policy-makers. Idealistic statements in the UN can peacefully coexist with continuing military ties and growing economic involvement.

There is no sign that the Nixon Administration feels ill at ease with any of these forces. Henry Kissinger, the President's principal foreign policy adviser, is the author of an important book on NATO which does not mention Portugal at all. The Nixon foreign policy report of February 1970 also failed to mention Portuguese colonialism in particular, but in the context of Southern Africa reaffirmed the bases of American policy: a ritual affirmation of racial equality and self-determination, combined with the qualification that 'we cannot agree that progressive change in Southern Africa is furthered by force'.

The possibility exists, moreover, of moves to increase co-operation with Portugal. The negotiations on the Spanish bases have been concluded (in spite of protests from the Senate Foreign Relations Committee), and the way is now open for negotiations on the status of the bases in the Azores. The Center for Strategic and International Studies, at Georgetown University, which has close connections with the Navy, has recently published a handbook on Portuguese Africa. Of the editors, one is now engaged in organizing for the Center a conference on South Africa's role in the Indian Ocean, in cooperation with South African government officials. The other, David Abshire, is now Assistant Secretary of State for Legislative Affairs. In a section of the handbook entitled 'Emerging Policies and Alternatives', he writes as follows:

there is little doubt that Portuguese rule will continue in the foreseeable future. But this does not mean a static situation, for the Portuguese have initiated a vast educational revolution for Africans. Thus, valuable time is being bought, and this will allow for development. At a later date, there should be a better chance for the proper application of the principle of self-determination, applied at the right time and in the right circumstance. Effective representation – true self-government – necessitates choice, under circumstances in which it can be intelligent and meaningful. . . . In the coming crucial decade of educational development, if there can truly be a coequal assimilation of African and Portuguese values, in a way that appreciates both rich heritages, Angola and Mozambique might take their places in tropical Africa as free and stable societies.

(*Portuguese Africa*, p. 464)

The handbook presents itself as unbiased and 'dispassioned'. The direction of the writers' sympathies is nevertheless clearly Portuguese.

There does exist, however, a minority opinion within the foreign policy elite. For those specifically concerned with Africa, the contradiction between the formal commitment to self-determination and the actual ties to white Southern Africa is felt more acutely. The United States has political and economic interests in independent black Africa as well, where the sentiment (if not always the practical commitment) argues for the full liberation of the African continent from white rule. Thus many of those who have day-to-day responsibilities for dealing with Africa, thinking in longer-range terms, tend to feel that in the long run the commitment to white Southern Africa may be self-destructive for American interests.

One of the representatives of such a viewpoint is Waldemar Nielsen, former President of the African-American Institute, which has served several government agencies (including the CIA) in dealing with African students. His recent book *The Great Powers and Africa*, and the earlier *African Battleline*, both stem from discussion groups in the Council on Foreign

Relations, and must be taken as representing a significant, if still a minority, view among the foreign policy elite. The participants in the study groups preceding *The Great Powers and Africa* included General Andrew J. Goodpaster, now commander of NATO, as well as others influential in American foreign policy (see Appendix).

In 1965 Nielsen suggested use of American pressure to bring about 'some progressive modification of Portuguese policy', in the hopes that 'this might well be sufficient to restrain the more extreme and dangerous tendencies on the African side' (*African Battleline*, p. 35). At the same time, he rejected sanctions and defined the task of American diplomacy as follows:

first, to develop contact and communication with those political groups presently not in control of government but likely to assume control in the future, in order to exert some influence on the character of the regimes they will establish; second, during the period of political transformation, to attempt to 'assure the freedom of the revolution' by helping to reduce or counter those internal or external factors which could frustrate evolutionary change and lead to violence and disruption; and third, during this hazardous and inflamed transitional stage nonetheless to attempt to maintain workable relations with existing regimes in order to assist transition and to protect current American interests and objectives.

(*African Battleline*, p. 139)

The scholarship programme of the African-American Institute was one instrument designed to build contacts with those who would be the future rulers. So was the establishment of schools for refugees in Tanzania and Zambia. The dissatisfaction of both students and liberation movements with these programmes, as well as the continuing American support for Portugal, has meant that hardly anyone has taken them as signs of sincere American identification with the liberation struggle. American influence in the Congo has also implied continued American ties with the Kinshasa-based GRAE. But compared to American ties with Portugal, such African ties are minor.

In *The Great Powers and Africa*, Nielsen suggests a re-examination of American attitudes to white Southern Africa:

leading, he hints, even to Portugal's exclusion from NATO, or restriction on the flow of American private investment. He also continues the theme of non-military aid to the liberation movements, thus 'checking the drift of the nationalist movements into bitterness, extremism, and growing dependence on Communist support' (p. 358). Such a policy, he argues, would create in the future greater American leverage on both sides that could be exerted towards a peaceful compromise settlement.

Such a shift in policy by the United States could, in so far as ties with Portugal were really broken, open up opportunities for the liberation struggle, as a wedge was driven between Portugal and the United States, and Portugal was consequently weakened. But in so far as such a policy simply led to an increase in the American search for a 'moderating' influence within the liberation movements, it would pose additional dangers for them, and an impediment to their aims.

This kind of change in American policy is unlikely to be more than an emergency 'fallback' position, as long as the possibility of maintaining the *status quo* appears to policymakers a live option. The three reasons that Nielsen gives for his proposed changes give as well some clues to the conditions under which they might be accepted. He talks of ideals; of the necessity to keep out extremist and communist influence; and of the divisive danger in this country of black and youth reaction to another Vietnam in Southern Africa.

The drive to consistency with ideals, particularly the ones of racial equality and self-determination, hardly seems likely to produce a change in policy, given past experience with American policy in Africa, and elsewhere. And the fear of 'extremism' will be seriously activated, one may predict, only when policymakers envisage the likelihood of substantial gains by the liberation movements. The escalation of the struggle in Southern Africa also seems to be a prerequisite for focusing substantial attention among blacks and radicals in the United States on what is happening there.

If, then, the United States ever does move in the direction advocated by Nielsen, cutting down support for Portugal and seeking actively for influence among the new rulers, it will be in response to the advance of the armed struggle which the people of Angola, Mozambique, and Guinea-Bissau are now waging. American policy may also be pushed in that direction by whatever solidarity with that struggle develops within the United States. If such a change does come, moreover, these same two factors will determine the possibilities for using it to the advantage of the struggle and defeating the attempts at manipulation.

The struggle of the peoples of Angola, Mozambique, and Guinea-Bissau is not just an isolated fight against an anachronistic colonial power. As they have fought, they have discovered that they fight also against white rule in Southern Africa as a whole; and that they are joined by allies from South Africa, from Zimbabwe and Namibia. They have discovered that they fight also against an imperial system, in which many countries are involved and of which the United States is the head. They fight knowing that others struggle against the same enemy, in Asia, in Latin America, in the Middle East, and even in the heart of the system, in the United States of America.

9 New Developments 1970-71

The War Continues

As the war against Portuguese colonialism in Africa moves into its second decade, the Portuguese counter-insurgency forces have undertaken several major new steps in the attempt to re-impose colonial stability. Although unsuccessful, these actions have helped to move the struggle to a higher level. The invasion of Guinea–Conakry, the use of herbicides in Angola, the massive 'search and destroy' offensives in Mozambique – all have been countered by the liberation forces which are renewing the attack on the Portuguese with new intensity and with increased international support.

On 22 November 1970, a Portuguese-led force including Africans drafted into the Portuguese army and dissidents from Guinea–Conakry attacked Conakry from the sea. The intent was to topple the regime of Sekou Touré, which has given consistent support to the liberation struggle in Guinea-Bissau, and to replace it by a regime disposed to deny 'sanctuary' to the PAIGC guerrilla forces. Among the targets of attack was the PAIGC office in Conakry, and the prison where Portuguese soldiers taken prisoner by PAIGC were kept. As was confirmed by a UN investigation and by a detailed account obtained secretly by PAIGC from Portuguese sources, the attack was planned and carried out by Portuguese authorities. If successful, it would have been a blow to the liberation struggle. But it failed, and thus helped to rally new support in Africa, and a new awareness of the struggle going on in Guinea-Bissau. Contributions to the OAU liberation fund have gone up. Nigeria has proposed that certain African states take responsibility for freeing at least one colonial territory in three years, and a West African office of the OAU Liberation Committee has been set up in Conakry.

Meanwhile PAIGC has stepped up its own offensive. A communiqué released in July 1971 reported PAIGC artillery and infantry attacks on the two major urban centres still held by the Portuguese, Bissau (the capital), and Bafata. These reports are confirmed by an article in the Conservative *Daily Telegraph* of London (5 August 1971). In it Bruce Loudon reports that in Lisbon 'with dramatic speed ... nonchalance about the situation in Guinea has changed to concern ... the guerrillas ... are attacking on an unprecedentedly big scale'. The direct attacks on Bissau and Bafata, noted the PAIGC communiqué, 'mark a new stage in the politico-military evolution of our national liberation struggle'.

In the sparsely populated regions of eastern Angola, where the liberation struggle is most intense, the Portuguese have since 1970 made extensive use of herbicides and napalm in attempts to destroy the crops grown by the people. In spite of these reprisals MPLA has been able to maintain guerrilla action over a wide area in the east, and to push into Bié, in central Angola, as well as continuing fighting at a lower level of intensity in Cabinda and in the north.

With its support in the urban area of Luanda as well, and its extensive educational, medical, and development programmes, MPLA has a broad base for advancing the liberation struggle. Its coherent strategy and discipline have won it new support from the OAU Liberation Committee, and others sympathetic to the liberation of Angola.

In Mozambique the series of offensives launched under the leadership of General Kaulza de Arriaga have been followed by Portuguese claims, in 1970 and again in 1971, that FRELIMO has been 'wiped out'. But the Portuguese took heavy losses, and failed to do more than destroy a number of fixed installations. As FRELIMO's President Samora Machel told the editor of the *Tanzanian Nationalist* (visiting inside Mozambique in May 1971),

The offensive was extremely important to FRELIMO. It was important because it constituted the first real test for us. It revealed the level of development of our struggle. The fact that we were able to confront victoriously 40,000 Portuguese soldiers equipped with the most modern weapons demonstrates that our struggle has reached a stage where it can no longer be defeated.

FRELIMO has succeeded subsequently in stepping up attacks in the crucial Tete province, close to the Cabora Bassa construction. And an advance south of the Zambezi has been admitted in Portuguese communiqués. The Portuguese hoped to maintain the Zambezi as a natural barricade, but have failed, as is illustrated even in their own propaganda.

And while fighting in Africa escalates, the Portuguese regime is now confronted with a fourth front as well, in Portugal itself. Desertion from the Portuguese army, draft evasion (by immigration to France or other countries), and student dissent against the war is not new in Portugal. But the pace seems to have stepped up, and with the organization of Armed Revolutionary Action (ARA), a new element has been added – effective sabotage actions. Beginning in November 1970, with explosions aboard ships bound for the African wars, ARA has destroyed a dozen aircraft at the Tancos Air Force base, shut off Lisbon telecommunications during the May 1971 NATO conference, sabotaged an ammunition ship off the Mozambique coast, and blown up a major ammunition dump in Santarem, Portugal. Premier Caetano, in a speech of 2 April 1971, stressed the danger to Portugal from internal subversion, noting that 'in the metropole a fifth column is working for them [the African guerrillas]! Never forget that!' Portugal's rulers have no intention of ending the war, but their difficulties, in Africa and internally, are mounting.

Imperial Contradictions

While the wars in Portuguese Africa have continued and escalated, the international context of those wars has been affected by two contradictory developments. On the one hand, the expansion of American, European, and South African interests in Portugal and its colonies has continued – the imperial network becomes ever more intricate, and Portugal gets renewed support. On the other hand, the possibility of isolating Portugal from some of her allies has become a more viable option. The coincidence of Portuguese colonial interests and Western neo-colonial interests draws them closer together. But action by progressive forces in the West together with the continued success of the liberation forces creates the possibility of cutting off at least some part of the Western support for Portuguese colonialism.

Increased American support for Portuguese colonialism is reflected in the Nixon administration's decision to allow the sale of two Boeing 707s to Portugal for use in troop transport. Although planes sold to the Portuguese airline (TAP) have in the past served the same purpose, this new sale is distinctive in that the planes are explicitly for troop transport. Still in the old style of deception are the quadrupled exports of herbicides to Portugal in 1970, with a denial that they are being used in Africa; and sales of five Bell helicopters to the Zambezi Development Office in Mozambique, for ostensibly civilian use only. In November 1970, six Portuguese army lieutenants, having deserted from the Portuguese army, testified that they had been trained in West Germany by US guerrilla warfare experts, before being sent to Mozambique. In March 1971, American officers participated in a special training course in Lisbon for Portuguese officers. During the summer Agnew ended up his world tour of 'friendly' nations with a visit to Portugal.

The pro-Portuguese stance of NATO has been confirmed by the selection (in June 1971) of Foreign Minister Joseph Luns, of the Netherlands, as the new Secretary-General. Luns has been a consistent supporter of Portugal's colonial wars, recently replying to criticism by affirming that 'Portugal sheds its blood for our freedom'. The editor of NATO's magazine *Fifteen Nations* goes even further, and advocates NATO cooperation with South Africa as well (*South Africa Digest*, 6 August 1971).

Britain's friendship for Portugal has been reconfirmed under the Conservative government. A Conservative study group, the Conservative Commonwealth and Overseas Council, had in

1970 noted the role of Angola and Mozambique as 'buffers' in Southern Africa, as well as the strategic importance of the Cape Verde Islands. It suggested that 'it would seem fully appropriate to reverse the present unfriendly policy and come to some arrangement with our Portuguese ally'. At the end of May 1971, Sir Alec Douglas-Home, British Foreign Secretary, visited Lisbon, a gesture characterized by the London *Financial Times* as a 'vote of confidence' in Portugal.

There have been no major new developments in French and German support for Portuguese colonialism. But for several reasons that support has become more visible. Apart from South Africa, French, and German companies are the most significant participants in the Cabora Bassa project, and have proved resistant to African protests at their involvement. France's role in supplying South Africa and Portugal with arms has been attacked openly by the O A U. But, far from reversing its position, France has cooperated with South Africa in promoting 'dialogue', which has been embraced by such French-influenced states as the Ivory Coast and the Malagasy Republic. The Malagasy Republic in particular is developing close ties with South Africa, and a shipbuilding project in Narinda harbour there (with South African, French, and Portuguese collaboration) is being considered. As for Germany, recent reports of the use of G-91 jet fighters in Mozambique point to the continued importance of West German military aid. And indications of West German ties with the Portuguese invasion of Guinea have been revealed by Conakry authorities.

It is South African involvement, however, that seems to be growing most rapidly. As construction on the Cabora Bassa scheme has begun to face threats from F R E L I M O guerrillas, the open involvement of South African troops has become more imminent. Michael Morris, a member of the Security Branch of the South African Police, writes in a recent book (*Terrorism*, p. 173) of the 'possibility of a South African military-defensive presence at Cabora. . . . We have very positively to impress upon the Portuguese authorities that we should have a South African military force at Tete, and we should do so openly.' He goes on to reveal that such forces are already there clandestinely by saying,

> By the way, it should not be assumed that the calling, in this chapter, for such things, is in any way a statement that such things definitely do not occur or are not existent. Oh no! It should be seen more as a call to act openly.

On the Angolan eastern front, South African helicopters, manned by South Africans, play an increasingly important role. According to Josef Raab, of the *Frankfurter Rundschau* (4 June 1971),

> The airport at Luso (military headquarters for the eastern zone) has been extended in a joint operation between Portuguese and South African technicians. According to informed circles the project was realized to a large extent with German capital.

Western capital, and South African and Portuguese military, thus cooperate in the counter-insurgency effort.

South Africa is also increasing its economic role. While this has always been important, involvement in Angola is just beginning a significant stage of expansion. A statement by a South African executive at the December 1969 conference of the South African Foreign Trade Organization is typical of the country's attitude:

> We have now talked about influencing factors in establishing a permanent foothold and will give you some quick personal thoughts on what might be the ideal establishment in Angola. Capital structure, South Africa, 70%; local capital, 30%. Members of the Board, two South African directors, resident South Africa; one South African resident in Angola; one director from the raw material source in Angola, for example steel, which holds incidentally a monopoly supply position in certain fields, and one Portuguese director from one of the principal industrial and banking groups. The 30% share capital could be distributed among the resident South African director and the major local interests.... [By such an arrangement] You invest a minimum of capital in the territory, yet can take 70% of the profits and pass on a fair percentage of the problems. The import of the critical components of the product enable you to use your South African resources. ... [This] is the surest way of obtaining a permanent foothold in Angola.

The integration of South African, Portuguese, and other Western interests in the Portuguese colonies is strikingly revealed in the banking industry. In 1966 one of the largest Portuguese banks, the Banco Português do Atlántico, joined through its Angolan subsidiary with the South African company General Mining and Finance to form the Bank of Lisbon and South Africa. In 1971, an arrangement with Barclays Bank (one of the largest banks in South Africa and England) was negotiated in which Barclays established a holding in the Angolan subsidiary of the Banco Português do Atlántico, which in turn took over Barclays' branches in Mozambique. Earlier a joint arrangement between Banco Totta-Aliança and Standard Bank of South Africa had been worked out, to form Banco Totta-Standard in Angola and Mozambique. Standard Bank of South Africa is a leading British and South African bank, now 15 per cent owned by Chase Manhattan Bank of New York. Thus, in the crucial financial sector of the economy, diverse foreign interests are increasingly intertwined.

This integration of business and political interests among the different countries in the Western imperial network is embodied in personal as well as institutional ties. A glimpse at what these may be was given by former West German Minister of Defence Franz Josef Strauss, when he told the Angolan newspaper *O Comércio* in April 1971:

> During the ten years of my term in office, I always did all I could to keep our relations in Portugal as good as possible.

He added that he thought West Germany should offer more help, and in passing he mentioned that:

> On May 19 and 20 I will be in Lisbon with a group of friends which meets twice a year in various cities of the world. In the Portuguese capital the group will include the former President of France Antoine Pinay, David Rockefeller and the former Italian Minister of Defence Andreotti.

David Rockefeller is Chairman of the Chase Manhattan Bank, and of the Council on Foreign Relations.

But while Portuguese and Western ruling sectors continue to

solidify their good relationships, there are new hopes that Portugal might be isolated in its adamant pursuit of colonial counter-insurgency. These hopes surfaced most dramatically perhaps during the June 1970 conference in Rome in support of the peoples of the Portuguese colonies. That conference, attended by support groups from around the world, as well as the liberation movements themselves, stressed the importance of internationalizing the struggle against Portuguese colonialism. In a symbolic move, the Pope granted a brief audience to leaders of FRELIMO, MPLA, and PAIGC, causing a crisis between Portugal and the Vatican. Portugal's Ambassador was recalled, and although he later returned to Rome the hitherto close support for Portugal by the Catholic Church had been cracked, if not broken. Less than a year later, that relationship was further disturbed by the decision by the White Fathers missionary order to withdraw from Mozambique. In a public statement, the order condemned the refusal of the Portuguese hierarchy to take a position in the face of 'injustices and police brutalities'. The statement continued, 'Faced with a silence which we do not understand, we feel in conscience that we do not have the right to be included among the accomplices of the official support which the bishops, in this way, seem to give to a regime which shrewdly uses the Church to consolidate and perpetuate an anachronistic situation in Africa.'

On another front, the international campaign against Western involvement in the Cabora Bassa project achieved some success. African countries and Western European protest groups joined in condemning the involvement of specific companies, and Swedish and Italian companies were induced to withdraw. A British company decided not to participate, and, even in the United States, General Electric did not get its expected Export-Import Bank loan, and accordingly withdrew. In West Germany, although German companies maintained their participation, the campaign against them reached significant proportions. Thus, although Cabora Bassa construction went on with South African, French, and German involvement, to be stopped, it seemed, only by stepped-up FRELIMO attacks, the campaigns dealt a blow to Portugal's international position and brought the struggle against Portuguese colonialism to public attention.

One of the important results of this public attention was the increase in the number of groups and already established organizations deciding to give specific, material support to the liberation struggle. Of particular symbolic importance was the decision of the World Council of Churches to give material aid to liberation movements for the non-military programmes of the movements. In the controversy thus stirred up in the churches, the legitimacy of the struggle of the peoples of Southern Africa was reaffirmed. Similarly U N agencies, instructed by the General Assembly to organize aid for the liberation movements in Portuguese Africa, were beginning to match resolutions with concrete aid, in spite of opposition from the United States and other Western countries. Outside such official bodies, groups in almost all the countries whose governments and business circles aid Portuguese colonialism organized to provide a counter-support to the liberation movements.

In the United States the campaign against Gulf Oil took on much more prominence than that against involvement in Cabora Bassa. Gulf Oil's blatant support for Portugal through its involvement in Angola made it a ready target, and in 1970 and 1971 a variety of groups joined in making Gulf's annual meeting a focus of protests. That protest has failed to force Gulf Oil to withdraw, but its extension into a boycott holds promise of continuing the pressure, and at least spreading the realization that there is a war in Angola, and that American companies are helping to maintain Portuguese colonialism.

Of much greater potential significance for the future, however, is a rapidly growing, if still diffuse, awareness among black Americans of the struggle in Southern Africa. The barrier built up and maintained by the bias of media and educational institutions is being broken down, and many are moving from an awareness of identification with Africa to more specific knowledge of and concern with struggles in Africa. From the Black Caucus of Congress to the Black Panthers or the League of

Revolutionary Black Workers, and within a wide spectrum of other groups, this awareness is beginning to move towards concrete links between the struggle here and the struggle there. American support for Portuguese colonialism and racism in Southern Africa still places this country squarely against liberation in Southern Africa. But there may well be building up a more significant challenge to that support, a force which may blunt it, and throw new weight to the forces of liberation. Meanwhile, *a luta continua* – the struggle continues.

10 The Nixon Doctrine:
What Role for Portugal?

Trends in US Policy

After almost five years of Nixon foreign policy, a significant shift in American policy towards the white regimes of Southern Africa is unmistakably clear, although there is still a basic continuity in official statements. Thus, David Newsom, Assistant Secretary of State for African Affairs, has affirmed in speeches around the country that 'the US government has consistently supported the principle of self-determination for all peoples in Africa', and that 'we have consistently favored peaceful change in Southern Africa through supporting constructive alternatives to the use of force' (*Milwaukee Journal*, 4 March 1973). Such pious statements, combined with continuing tacit support for the *status quo*, are certainly no innovation, but behind the verbal façade of continuity basic changes are at work, integrating ever more closely US policy with support of the white regimes. Even though National Security Council documents outlining US strategy are classified, it is possible to judge the direction of policy from the limited information that has become available publicly.

Vetoes in the United Nations, the violation of United Nations sanctions against Rhodesia by importing chrome, the appointment of Texas oilman John Hurd as Ambassador to South Africa – all are signs of the new approach of more 'communications', a cosier relationship with the white regimes. Perhaps most blatant is the support given to Portuguese colonialism by the renewal of the Azores base agreement. The last formal agreement concerning US use of this base lapsed in 1962 (see pages 108–9, above), although interim arrangements maintained US involvement intact. President Nixon's decision to renegotiate a formal agreement represents a decision to publicly identify with and support the Portuguese regime. In concrete terms, the December 1971 accord obtained two more years for the US base in the Azores, in exchange for unprecedented aid to Portugal. Included was $30 million under the PL 480 'Food for Peace' programme, $1 million for education, a waiver of $175,000 in annual payments for the US Military Assistance Advisory Group, an oceanographic vessel, $5 million for non-military surplus equipment, and, most striking, access to $400 million in Export-Import Bank credits. The $400 million exceeded the total Eximbank credits to Portugal from the Second World War until 1970 by a margin of over $300 million. In comparison, the whole African continent (excluding South Africa) has received only slightly more than $350 million in Eximbank loans during the same period. The same figure of $400 million is approximately equal to Portugal's total military budget, and while the loans were not directly for military purposes, they represented an important boost to the Portuguese government precisely when Premier Caetano was calling on Portuguese citizens to accept slower growth at home in order to finance the continuing colonial wars.

Of more direct military significance is the erosion of controls on exports of 'civilian aircraft' to Portugal for use in the wars in Africa. Prior to 1970, aircraft supplied to the Portuguese airlines (TAP), some paid for with Eximbank credits, were already being used for troop transport. Between 1966 and 1970 Eximbank credits or guarantees were provided for five Boeing 707s, three Boeing 727s, and four Boeing 747s. In late 1970 two Boeings were sold directly to the Portuguese government with the clear understanding that they were to be used for troop transport. In 1971 two more 747s were reported purchased by TAP, again for troop transport. More recently, the Portuguese airline in Mozambique, DETA, has purchased a series of at least four 737s. A recent announcement noted that

DETA had acquired a flight simulator for training pilots (who had previously been sent to the US for training). David Newsom noted in a letter to John Marcum dated 8 October 1971 that, 'Though these air and freight services can obviously carry military as well as civilian passengers, the sale of passenger transport planes to Portugal has not been deemed to come within the terms of our 1961 arms embargo.' The military significance of these planes is nevertheless very substantial. With long lines of communication between Portugal and Africa, and within Africa – especially from south to north within Mozambique – Portuguese logistic problems, as well as the problem of the morale of soldiers so far away from their families, are substantially lessened by the availability of jet transport.

The sale of other smaller planes is more difficult to trace, but it is clear that within the last year there have been at least two major sales to Portuguese authorities in Mozambique. One, revealed in testimony before the Subcommittee on Africa of the House Foreign Affairs Committee (Judge William H. Booth and Ms Jennifer Davis, 22 March 1973), involved three Shrike Commanders and one Aero Commander, sold by North American Rockwell to a Mozambican company for aerial photo-reconnaissance in northern Mozambique, the location of FRELIMO's longest established liberated areas. The other was a sale of twelve helicopters to the Communications Department of the Portuguese government in Mozambique. Further details of the second sale are not yet available, but several US companies appear to have been involved in the initial bidding.

These specific steps of support for the Portuguese government have been accompanied by continued smaller signs – visits from the National War College to observe the wars in Angola and Mozambique, visits by US Navy ships to Luanda and Lourenço Marques, reports that National Security Council facilities in Kagnew, Ethiopia, are being used to monitor the movements of forces in the wars in Southern Africa, and that the information is being shared with the

Portuguese military. Clark MacGregor, former official of President Nixon's re-election campaign and now a vice-president of United Aircraft, made a trip to Rhodesia, Angola, and Mozambique in late 1972, reporting that he was happy to confirm all the fine things he understood constituted Portuguese policy in Africa (quoted in *Africa Report*, January-February 1973, 'In Washington'). His tour included a visit to northern Mozambique, and he reported to the President on his return to the United States.

The fact of increased collaboration with the Portuguese regime should be beyond dispute, in spite of State Department denials that there has been a change of policy. Terence Smith, in a *New York Times* article of 2 April 1972, revealed that the policy shift was no mere drift natural to a conservative administration, but a deliberate policy embodied in a National Security Council position paper (still classified). According to Smith, three options were considered: the 'Dean Acheson' option for open ties with the white regimes, ignoring their racial policies; the 'more of the same' option of continuing the Kennedy-Johnson limited dissociation from the white regimes; and the 'tarbaby' option, calling for increased communication and selective involvement with the white governments, including attempts to persuade them to bring about limited modifications in their policies. The decision to adopt the third position was made in January 1970, but even the fact that the decision had been taken was kept quiet.

The detailed rationale behind the decision is unavailable to the public, but it is possible to get an outline from the general contours of 'Nixon Doctrine' foreign policy, and more particularly from an article by David M. Abshire, who went from his position at the Center for Strategic and International Studies at Georgetown University to Assistant Secretary of State for Congressional Relations under President Nixon. In general, the new Nixon foreign policy involves three elements: (1) 'partnership' – the attempt to shift the burden of maintaining stability in the different regions of the world to reliable partners (the Thieu regime, Iran, Brazil, and others), making use of non-American military forces as much as possible; (2) 'negotiation' – the attempt to reach agreements with the Soviet Union and the People's Republic of China, and to seek to persuade them to cut off or limit support for revolutionary forces in the Third World; (3) 'strength' – the continuing determination to use whatever strength is necessary, including American military forces if no other alternative is available, to maintain a stability conducive to continued access by American business and military.

The implementation of this strategy is apparent in the continued attempt to maintain hegemony in Indochina through more covert support of the Thieu regime and the bombing in Cambodia. It is also apparent in the military sales by the US to Kuwait and Iran, in the strategic, oil-rich Gulf region. Again, in Latin America, the role of Brazil as a regional power and the continued ties with Latin American military establishments fit within the general strategy. That the limited retreat from Indochina does not mean an abdication of the American imperial role is well documented in Michael Klare's recent book, *War Without End*: *American Planning for the Next Vietnams*. There the strategies being developed to continue counter-insurgency without the heavy use of American troops are spelled out in detail.

What then is the application of this general strategy to Southern Africa, and to the Portuguese colonies in particular? American policy-makers seem to have made three basic judgements: (1) Southern Africa is of strategic importance to the United States; (2) the best guarantee of stability on Western terms can be found in cooperation with the existing, white-dominated regimes; (3) those regimes, in order to become more acceptable and more effective partners in maintaining stability, would be well advised to make some limited steps towards greater participation by Africans. There are two corollary judgements: (1) the disruptive 'liberation movements' must be contained while the reforms are given time to work, and (2) the cooperation with the white regimes must be 'low-key' so as to minimize international criticism and domestic debate about the issue.

As seen by US policy-makers, the strategic significance of Southern Africa rests both on its role as the most prosperous and mineral-rich section of Africa and on its key location *vis-à-vis* the sea route from the Atlantic to the oil of the Middle East. Southern Africa (including Zambia and Zaire) produces more than 10 per cent of world production of the following minerals: gold (69 per cent in 1969), gem diamonds (64 per cent in 1969), industrial diamonds (64 per cent in 1969), contained cobalt (57 per cent in 1969), chromite (32 per cent in 1969), vanadium (29 per cent in 1969), platinum (28 per cent in 1969), vermiculite (31 per cent in 1969), antimony (28 per cent in 1969), copper (22 per cent in 1969), contained uranium (17 per cent in 1969), manganese (14 per cent in 1969), and beryllium (10 per cent in 1969). While it may be contended that none of these are absolutely essential to the US economy their importance to both military and corporate planners is unmistakable. David Abshire notes that 'if by the term "strategic" we mean to include the range of economic forces that mesh with the political, technological, and military to develop or undermine great-power influence, African resources are certainly strategic' (*Portuguese Africa*, p. 434).

Abshire's article also emphasizes the strategic role of the Portuguese possessions. Metropolitan Portugal, Madeira, and the Azores, he notes, form a strategic triangle in the North Atlantic, significant for control both of a substantial portion of the Atlantic and of the gateway to the Mediterranean. He sees Cape Verde as a centre-post of the ocean between Latin America and Africa, as well as a possible base for 'airlift of the forces of any great power into Africa'. While Angola's mineral wealth has great potential, Abshire emphasizes its role as controller of the mouth of the Congo River. Because of its position, according to Abshire, in the event of further disorder in the Congo (Zaire), Angola could serve as a base of operations to restore order. Mozambique's significance relates primarily to the role of the Indian Ocean in US naval strategy, a role which stems from the necessity to keep control of the transportation routes for Arab/Persian Gulf oil. Abshire comments in passing that the new port of Nacala, in Mozambique, 'is so large that it could accommodate the entire US Seventh Fleet'.

In terms of these strategic interests, and on the basis of a concept of stability which means continued access by Western business, it makes sense to stick with the white regimes. The aid to Portugal described above is not then just the remnant of an old alliance, but is an integral part of a current plan in which Portugal plays its role in keeping global 'law and order'. As Abshire observes (p. 462), 'there is little doubt that Portuguese rule will continue in the foreseeable future. . . . At a later date, there should be a better chance for the proper application of the principle of self-determination, applied at the right time and in the right circumstance.' The strategic line is thus support for the Portuguese presence, and, as a corollary, opposition to the use of force by the liberation movements fighting against Portuguese rule.

But there must be some recognition of the fact that a hard consistent line against African majority rule not only runs into trouble with the United Nations and a growing constituency in the United States, but also impedes the most efficient prosecution of the counter-insurgency effort. Support for the Portuguese is thus combined with emphasis on the possibilities of advance towards African participation within the Portuguese system, and even (on occasion) with votes in the United Nations criticizing Portugal (as long as no implementation is implied). Abshire reveals in his concluding pages that he shares some elements of the Portuguese vision for their African colonies, and urges continuing development of Angola and Mozambique within that context:

The hope for increased representative government, and even, eventually, African majority rule will probably be found in the leverage that Africans, within ten years, will themselves be exercising by means of the present establishment rather than through the divided and disorganized nationalist groups with tribal biases.

As Portuguese rule moves in these directions, the hope is evidently that support for such a Lusitanian Commonwealth might prove less a political liability than would support for obvious Portuguese colonialism, and would serve equally well as a means of defending US strategic interests.

How does this US strategy correspond with the Portuguese regime's own plans and possibilities? Does Portugal's own dependent position still prevent a transition to neo-colonialism, or is a new situation emerging? What changes are taking place in the methods being used to maintain the Portuguese colonial presence? Since whatever changes are taking place are likely to be used as cosmetic justifications for continued US support for Portugal, it is important to understand just what they do and do not mean.

Portugal's Neo-Colonial Option

It is clear, first of all, that on the formal level some changes have already taken place. The 'Organic Law for the Overseas' of May 1972 resulted in renaming Angola and Mozambique 'states' instead of 'provinces', and in the establishment of new legislative assemblies in all the African colonies. There is a redistribution of governmental responsibilities, with more falling under the jurisdiction of the legislative assemblies. However, the executive responsibility in each territory is still lodged with the Governor, appointed by the government in Lisbon. Moreover, the Portuguese Overseas Minister retains the power to revoke or annul all or part of the legislation enacted in the territories when such legislation is unconstitutional, illegal, or 'contrary to the higher interests of the State'. The reforms then represent a greater degree of possible access or influence for those in the territories who are allowed to participate. However, the basic authority, even in legal terms, remains with the metropolitan Portuguese regime.

In considering the legislative assemblies that have emerged, or other elections that may take place in the Portuguese territories, it is important to remember several basic facts about the Portuguese political system: the legislative branch has little independent role, elections are controlled by the official government party, and the franchise is extremely restricted, especially in the African territories, by requirements which include literacy. Nevertheless, the elections held in March 1973 for the legislative assemblies in the territories are important because for the first time they set up a limited façade of 'multi-racial' rule. Greater numbers of voters were registered by the authoritites (civil servants are automatically eligible for registration), including, according to Portuguese claims, a majority of non-whites in Angola and a substantial percentage of non-whites in Mozambique. In Mozambique, again according to Portuguese sources, 26 of the 50 candidates (all government-chosen) are non-white. Further evidence that image and not power is the crucial factor is provided by noting that only 20 of the 50 seats in Mozambique were elected by direct suffrage (only 32 out of 53 in Angola, and 5 out of 17 in Guinea-Bissau). The figures on voting are even more striking: in Angola approximately 500,000 out of a population of almost 6 million; in Mozambique 100,000 out of a population of almost 8 million; in Guinea-Bissau 8,000 out of a population of 600,000. Particularly striking in the case of Guinea-Bissau is the comparison with PAIGC's elections for a national assembly, held last year in the liberated areas of that country. In spite of the fact that Portuguese still hold the larger towns, over 77,000 voted in the elections held by PAIGC, almost ten times as many as voted in the Portuguese-sponsored election. A good proportion of those voting in the Portuguese-sponsored election, moreover, were undoubtedly government employees, for whom refusal to vote would be suspect.

If the elections must be regarded largely as a façade, with a very limited capacity to deceive large numbers of Africans in the Portuguese territories, other steps taken at the same time have more serious import as moves in the direction of neo-colonialism. These are the attempt to shift more of the burden of the war, both financial and human, to the African territories, and the drastic steps taken to readjust balance of payment problems between Portugal, Angola, and Mozambique.

The trend in recent years has been for an increasing proportion of war expenses to be paid out of the budgets of the African territories. That is one reason for the heightened importance of such investments as that of Gulf Oil in Angola, which provide revenue for those budgets. Nevertheless, Angola in particular, and Mozambique to some extent, have additional capacity to pay for the war, and it is the Portuguese intention to transfer even more of the burden to those budgets, which now account for approximately one-third of the military expenses. This implies, of course, a continuing lesser priority for non-military-related social expenditures, in spite of expressed goals of winning over the people by such measures.

The forced recruitment of Africans into the Portuguese Army is an even more ominous development for the liberation forces. This is not entirely a new development: Angolans from other parts of Angola were used in the counter-insurgency actions in northern Angola in the early 1960s. But the scale of the efforts is new, almost amounting to an Africanization of the lower ranks of the military. According to Portuguese claims, as much as 50 per cent of the armed forces may now be African. One such African, a deserter who joined FRELIMO in 1972, noted that many of the 'recruits' were coming 'directly from the prisons, and conscripted into the army' (*Mozambique Revolution*, October–December 1972). The recruitment of African conscripts, who are put in situations that make it extremely difficult for them to desert, is accompanied by psychological warfare which attempts to portray the liberation movements as 'terrorist' organizations engaged in attacking civilian populations. According to FRELIMO reports, this has gone so far as massacring civilians (even reports by Portuguese priests confirm a number of these actions), and then trying to publicize the massacres as FRELIMO's responsibility.

The economic steps taken towards a different relationship between Portugal and its colonies are also of substantial importance. The absence of exchange controls between Portugal and the colonies has meant substantial trade concentration, in a classical colonial pattern already described in Chapter 1. However, the currency systems have been maintained distinct, and it has been necessary to transfer payments from African currency into metropolitan Portuguese currency. In recent years, Angola and Mozambique have built up a large deficit on payments with Lisbon, with the result that metropolitan exporters, although enjoying the benefits of a protected market, were experiencing extreme delays in getting their payments. Last year the Portuguese government responded by imposing exchange controls, severely limiting imports into Portuguese Africa to those which could be paid for by exports. Results already apparent include a declining percentage of imports coming from Portugal, and new incentives for local Portuguese interests in Angola and Mozambique to establish processing industries to replace the imports.

It is almost impossible to determine which Portuguese business interests will suffer from the new arrangements and which will ultimately benefit. It is of particular interest, however, that some of the larger companies, such as DIAMANG in Angola, are reported to be exempt from many of the controls. Moreover, although Portuguese capital remains weak in such major sectors as mining, its strength lies precisely in those sectors of industry which may benefit. Moreover, the continued rapid expansion of Portuguese banks in Angola and Mozambique (most recently the formation of Banco Inter Unido, a joint operation of Banco Espírito Santo and First National City Bank of New York, was closely followed by the opening of its offices in Luanda) gives to those interests the possibility of taking a leading role in whatever development does take place in Angola and Mozambique outside the sectors dominated by non-Portuguese capital. Perhaps the basis for a neo-colonial financial network is being laid.

But if it is important to recognize the extent to which

elements of such a neo-colonial option are being prepared (perhaps most actively in Mozambique, where persistent rumours link General Kaulza de Arriaga and industrialist J. Jardim to preparations for a Rhodesian-style independence with participation by some Mozambican Africans), it is also important to recognize the limitations placed on the development of these options. These include the continued military significance of metropolitan Portugal for counter-insurgency action, the lack of willingness in Lisbon to relax real control, and the inability of such neo-colonial regimes to establish any international legitimacy as long as the liberation movements maintain and expand their present viability.

While the 'Africanization' discussed above does lessen somewhat the military burden on metropolitan Portugal, and while it is conceivable (especially in Mozambique) that South Africa could take up some of the slack left by a withdrawal of metropolitan Portuguese troops, any such withdrawal would for the foreseeable future cripple the Portuguese military effort. As long as the military effort involves metropolitan Portugal, moreover, the character of any local regime as a convenient façade remains readily apparent. The style of change, given the political character of the Portuguese regime, is more likely to resemble that of Caetano's earlier liberalization, which allowed a few token 'liberals' within the Portuguese National Assembly. Recently the two leaders of the liberal faction withdrew, claiming that they were only used to create a favourable image. In the words of Senhor Homen de Mello, a Caetano supporter, the two liberals did not respect the rules of the game: 'They behaved as though they were in a democratic system' (quoted in the *Daily Telegraph*, 13 March 1973). A similar fate undoubtedly awaits those Africans who attempt to follow Abshire's advice and advance the cause of majority rule through the 'present establishment'.

Certainly such manoeuvres are easily exposed when the liberation movements are advancing and building new societies in the areas which they gain control over. The social basis for their support is revealed in documents from the

Portuguese themselves. Thus Dr Afonso Mendes, in a confidential report on counter-insurgency based on extensive experience as Director of the Institute of Labour in Angola, noted 'the existence of grave "social lags", which are the origin of cracks through which subversive forces penetrate with their mission of disruption to win the sympathy of the malcontents. And in the case of Angola, these malcontents may constitute more than 90 per cent of the entire population!' (document obtained and published by the Angola Comité, Amsterdam). Faced with this reality, and with their failure to eliminate the liberation movements by ordinary military action, the Portuguese regime has set as a priority goal the disruption of the liberation movements by a campaign of infiltration and assassination.

Such efforts are not new. The assassination of Eduardo Mondlane in 1969 marked the culmination of one such campaign. But the recent campaign seems much more systematic and extensive and has already resulted in the death of another of Africa's great leaders, Amilcar Cabral of PAIGC, just on the eve of major steps forward in PAIGC's struggle. The plot (see the detailed description in *Southern Africa*, May 1973) involved the systematic infiltration into PAIGC of Portuguese agents, either former PAIGC members who had been won over while in prison, or agents sent to the PAIGC pretending to be deserters from the Portuguese forces. They were to win over or neutralize others in the party with the suggestion that the Portuguese would grant independence to Guinea alone, if PAIGC were destroyed, Cape Verdeans were excluded from any nationalist movement, and the Cape Verde islands were left for the Portuguese. Those involved in the plot succeeded in killing Cabral, but their attempt to kidnap other PAIGC leaders and turn them over to the Portuguese failed and the plotters were captured by the forces of Guinea (Conakry). In their confessions it was revealed that similar plots were under way against FRELIMO and MPLA.

In an interview some months following the assassination of

Cabral, President Samora Machel of FRELIMO (*Afrique-Asie* interview, 30 April 1973) commented on the tactics used by the Portuguese. He noted especially the use of ex-prisoners and infiltrators among the deserters from the Portuguese Army. 'On the basis of our personal experience,' he said, 'we know that in every hundred ex-prisoners or deserters, at least twenty-five to thirty are agents provocateurs.' Some of the difficulties involved in coping with such an offensive are easy to imagine. To pose rigid restrictions on the acceptance of such deserters in the party could cut off the flow of those who genuinely wish to desert from the colonial forces into which they were drafted; to exercise no control at all would be to expose the party to systematic destruction from within. Efficient security measures required to minimize mistakes must be well developed.

In spite of the serious Portuguese offensive against them, the liberation movements have made and are making important steps forward, both within each country and in the international arena. Neither clandestine Portuguese operations nor the more conventional counter-insurgency offensives have reversed the momentum against Portuguese colonialism and for liberation. In joining Portugal to help hold back the tide of freedom in Angola, Mozambique, and Guinea-Bissau, the United States is engaged in another exercise in futility.

The Liberation Struggle Continues to Advance

The timing of the assassination plot against Amilcar Cabral was no accident, for it came in the midst of preparations for the declaration of an independent state of Guinea-Bissau. Last year, a mission of the United Nations De-Colonization Committee visited the liberated areas of Guinea-Bissau. Later the same year, PAIGC-sponsored elections were held for a national assembly. In spite of the assassination, it is expected that the assembly will meet some time this year, declare Guinea-Bissau independent, and seek recognition (more than sixty states are expected to recognize the new government promptly) and membership in the United Nations. In the last General Assembly session, the United Nations granted special observer status to the liberation movements. If a US veto is avoided, and Guinea-Bissau is admitted this year, it will establish an important precedent. The legal situation will change from that of a Portuguese territory with an insurgent independence movement to an independent country with some of its territory occupied by a foreign power (Portugal). Such a legal change, although not altering the military situation inside Guinea-Bissau, would make possible greater international support for PAIGC from international agencies as well as individual countries.

It is important to note that plans for the meeting of the national assembly have been carried forward, although the assassination has undoubtedly led to even more careful security precautions than would ordinarily have been the case. Moreover, PAIGC has been stepping up military action against the Portuguese, for the first time making effective use of anti-aircraft weapons, using ground-to-air missiles to shoot down a number of Portuguese planes. The first plane shot down, in March, was that of the Portuguese Air Force commander in Guinea, who was killed. The death of Cabral was a serious loss for PAIGC and for Africa, but it has no more stopped the advance of the struggle in Guinea-Bissau than did the assassination of Mondlane in Mozambique four years ago.

The blows struck against the Portuguese in Guinea-Bissau are of particular importance because it is there that the struggle is furthest advanced, the Portuguese nearest to defeat. The advance of the struggle in Mozambique has another particular significance, that of the strategic location of Mozambique across important routes to the sea for Rhodesia and South Africa. Its common borders with both countries create the possibility for access by African guerrillas as FRELIMO penetrates farther south in Mozambique. Already guerrillas of ZANU have made use of FRELIMO-controlled access routes to begin effective guerrilla action in northeastern Zimbabwe (Rhodesia). Last year FRELIMO opened up a new front in

Manica and Sofala province, across the route from Salisbury to Beira. This year FRELIMO President Samora Machel announced that FRELIMO is beginning military operations in Zambezi province. These advances have caused consternation among the white regimes of Southern Africa, with the Rhodesians and South Africans accusing the Portuguese of doing an ineffective job of counter-insurgency, and debating whether to intervene more openly themselves. It has also prompted Malawi's President Banda to rethink his close ties with the white regimes, for he must consider the fact that Malawi's routes to the sea now run through FRELIMO-controlled areas.

While Angola's location makes it somewhat less strategically significant for South Africa and Rhodesia than is Mozambique, its mineral riches, both actual and potential, probably make it one of the most promising African countries in economic terms. In addition, its proximity to Zaire, emphasized by David Abshire, and its economic ties with the United States through Gulf Oil and through the sale of coffee, put it in a unique position among Portugal's African colonies. In the past the liberation struggle there has been severely hampered by the fact that MPLA, the leading movement, has been excluded from access to the long Zaire border, while the virtually inactive GRAE has enjoyed the monopoly of support from the Zaire government. MPLA operations have accordingly been concentrated in isolated Cabinda and in the sparsely populated east of Angola, accessible, in spite of tremendous logistical difficulties, from Zambia. Even in the east, the existence of a smaller movement, UNITA, not recognized by the Organization of African Unity, has prevented a fully unified mobilization of liberation forces. In spite of these difficulties, MPLA has continued to advance in military terms, last year repelling a strong Portuguese military offensive. But penetration into heavily populated western Angola has been slow. Therefore the recent agreement between MPLA and FNLA (National Front for Liberation of Angola, the liberation movement connected with the government-in-exile GRAE, which now goes out of existence) is of striking potential significance.

The agreement (signed in December 1972) seems to reflect discontent in the ranks of FNLA with the leadership of Holden Roberto, who has in the past resisted unity measures. It also seems to reflect a shift in policy by President Mobutu of Zaire, who is widely credited with inducing Holden Roberto to enter into the agreement. After six months it is still impossible to determine what it will actually mean. If it should mean combination of MPLA and FNLA forces for effective action in Angola from a Zaire base, the Portuguese would be immediately faced with a much more serious military threat in Angola than ever before. President Mobutu does seem to be moving towards a more Pan-African policy, and towards establishing contacts, for example, with the People's Republic of China. But his government's contacts with Portugal, and the large American military and economic role in Zaire, give cause for caution in predicting the extent of support the Angolan liberation struggle can expect from him. Zaire may well form a base for stepping up the Angolan liberation struggle ; Zambia, Senegal, and now perhaps even Malawi have played such roles in spite of the continued Western dominance of their economies. What happens in Zaire will have an important effect on stepping up, or slowing down, the advance of the liberation struggle in Angola.

While in all three African colonies the pressure on Portugal increases, opposition to the war within Portugal itself continues to express itself. The Portuguese 'opposition', allowed to meet occasionally this year in preparation for elections in the fall, has finally taken a consistent and strong stance in favour of ending the colonial war and negotiating with the liberation movements. While this kind of opposition has no possibility of making inroads in the controlled elections, or stepping much beyond the narrow restrictions imposed on its actions by the Portuguese police state, such a stance marks a shift in certain sectors of Portuguese opinion. The fact that priests in Mozambique have spoken out against the massacres committed by the Portuguese Army, in spite of the expected result of imprisonment, reveals some shift of thinking within the Church as well. Such shifts of opinion, as well as the continued draft evasion, are signs of a certain erosion of support for the war. However, they do not change the direction of policy, over which such public opinion has no influence. The more serious challenge, at least in hampering the colonial war effort, comes from groups such as ARA and, more recently, the Revolutionary Brigades, which have been organizing carefully planned sabotage against the Portuguese military machine. The seriousness of this threat is illustrated by the fact that the most recent bombings, in March 1973, were reported publicly even in the Portuguese military magazine, which noted in an editorial that 'the escalation of the attacks reveals the intention to open in Europe a "fourth front"'. The editorial went on to call for vigilance and intransigence against those elements who ally themselves with the enemies of Portugal in the overseas territories.

At the international level, the attempt to isolate Portugal has also met with some new successes, in spite of the stepped-up US support for Portugal. The UN General Assembly of 1972 seated representatives of the liberation movements as official observers, the first time such an action has been taken. The Security Council in November passed a resolution calling on Portugal to stop military action, enter into negotiations, and recognize the rights of self-determination of the people of its African colonies. Surprisingly, the resolution was passed unanimously, the Western powers evidently deciding to dissociate themselves at least to this extent from Portugal. Increasing support for the movements has come, moreover, from some of the smaller Western countries. Sweden has for a long time supported the movements, but now Norway, Denmark, and the Netherlands are joining as well. All three of the latter are members of NATO, and, together with Canada and Iceland, have pledged to raise the issue of Portuguese violence in its African colonies in the NATO council.

A crucial decision point, especially for the United States, will likely come in the fall of 1973, if, as expected, liberated Guinea-Bissau applies for United Nations membership. If the United States, France, or Great Britain veto the application, it will mean a clear decision to stand consistently with Portugal. If they abstain, or even vote in favour, it will mean a decision to accommodate at least to a minimal extent the undeniable advances of the liberation struggle. Similarly, it will be important to watch closely what happens in Zaire for clues to US strategy. Will the US position in Zaire be used to frustrate liberation movement advances, or will Zaire be used to strengthen a fall-back position of influencing any future Angolan government through Zaire and 'moderate' elements in FNLA?

Finally, as the war against Portuguese colonialism in Africa escalates, and as the liberation movements gain more and more access to more advanced weaponry – such as the missiles now being used in Guinea-Bissau – it will be important to watch for and work against escalated Western support for the Portuguese. Support in the United States and other Western countries for cutting off the white regimes is growing and is beginning to become significant, but in the major countries which form the bulwark of support for Portugal policy is still dominated by those forces bent on maintaining that support. It will require much more massive political education and mobilization of progressive forces before the rulers are forced to reconsider and change their position. As the liberation movements continue their struggle in Angola, Mozambique, Guinea-Bissau, and the rest of Africa still under white rule, the struggle here must also continue and expand.

Appendix
Membership of Council on Foreign Relations
Study Groups on Africa, 1966–8

Study Group on 'Western European, Soviet and Chinese Policy Toward Africa', 1966–7

Robert E. Asher, Brookings Institution
Col. Sidney Berry
Rep. Jonathan B. Bingham, Congressman (New York)
John A. Davis
William Diebold
W. D. Eberle, Chairman Urban America Inc.
J. Wayne Fredericks, Ford Foundation, formerly Dept of State
Rep. Peter H. B. Frelinghuysen, Congressman (New Jersey)
Gen. Andrew J. Goodpaster, NATO Commander-in-Chief
Robert Graff
Edward K. Hamilton
William A. Hance, Professor of Geography, Columbia University
James T. Harris, Jr, Ford Foundation, National Catholic
  Conference on Interracial Justice
Louis Henkin, Professor of Law, Columbia University
Graham Hovey, *New York Times*
Andrew M. Kamarck, Professor of Economics, Johns Hopkins
Ernest W. Lefever, Brookings Institution
Robert Lubar, *Fortune*
David W. MacEachron
Robert J. Manning, *Atlantic Monthly*
Robert Murphy, Morgan Guaranty Trust Company
Philip Quigg, *Foreign Affairs*
Rep. Ogden R. Reid, Congressman (New York)
Zelia Ruebhausen
Jo W. Saxe
R. Peter Straus, Straus Broadcasting Group (WMCA)
Francis X. Sutton, MIT
Willard L. Thorp, National Bureau of Economic Research

Carroll L. Wilson, Organization for Economic Cooperation and Development (OECD)

I. William Zartman, Professor, New York University, contributor to army study on counter-insurgency

Study Group on 'The Evolution of US Policy Toward Africa', 1968

Harry Boardman

Joseph E. Black, Rockefeller Foundation

Richard A. Falk, Professor of Law, Princetown University

Ernest A. Gross, lawyer, former assistant Secretary of State

Ambassador Fred L. Hadsel, Ambassador to Somalia

Edward K. Hamilton

Ulric Haynes, Jr

Roger Hilsman, Professor, Columbia University, former CIA, Department of State

Dan B. Lacy

William E. Lang, Department of Defense

George N. Lindsay, New York lawyer

Ian K. MacGregor, American Metal Climax mining company

John A. Marcum, author of *Angolan Revolution*

Ruth Schachter Morgenthau, author of a book on French West Africa

Herman J. Nissenbaum

George T. Percy

Philip Quigg, *Foreign Affairs*

Arnold Rivkin, MIT

Oscar Schachter, UN official

Immanuel Wallerstein, Professor of Sociology, Columbia University

Adam Yarmolinsky, Professor of Law, Harvard University, formerly Department of Defense

This Mobil ad was taken from the Portuguese military journal,
Jornal do Exército, November–December 1964. It shows
graphically the alliance between US corporations and the
Portuguese war machine. A translation of the ad reads:

IN THE GOOD HOURS AND THE BAD . . .
The wave of terrorism which treacherously attacked the
north of Angola imposed heroic sacrifices on the Armed
Forces and the people. Mobil, which has served the province since 1914, which pioneered in bringing to all areas
the petroleum products so important for its development,
which, in the good hours and the bad, always joined the
destiny of Angola and its people – Mobil could not be absent
from the sacrifices. Mobil has participated with pride in the
struggle for the defence of the province, pledging itself to
assure the supply of fuels and lubricants necessary for the
Armed Forces and the people.
MORE THAN HALF A CENTURY AT THE
SERVICE OF THE COUNTRY

This Jeep ad was taken from the March 1973 issue *Jornal do Exército*. According to *Business Week* (7 January 1967), Kaiser Jeep, now a subsidiary of American Motors, ranks as 'the world's largest manufacturer of tactical military vehicles'. A translation of the ad reads:

Willys Jeep – the name that made the all-terrain vehicle universal. Willys Jeep is the vehicle with the largest world production, the vehicle that has shown the best test results, that is the most resistant to wear. It is the 'all-terrain' vehicle preferred by the Armed Forces because of its incomparable resistance and versatility of application.

This Mercedes-Benz ad was taken from the February 1973 issue of *Jornal do Exército*. The caption reads:

> Military vehicles: the strongest and most efficient in all the services of the Armed Forces.

The caption is followed by a list of types of vehicles. Particularly interesting are the Unimog models, which in an earlier ad (November–December 1967) were identified as 'NATO' models.

Suggested Reading and Other Sources

James Duffy's book in the Penguin African Library, *Portugal in Africa* (Penguin Books, 1962) is the most important first book for those who want a more detailed picture of the history and character of Portuguese colonialism in Africa. His earlier book, *Portuguese Africa* (Harvard University Press, 1959), goes over much the same material in greater detail. C. R. Boxer's recent book *The Portuguese Seaborne Empire; 1415–1825* (Knopf, 1969) sums up the work of this distinguished historian of the early Portuguese Empire. *Portuguese Africa: A Handbook*, edited by David Abshire and Michael Samuels (Praeger, 1969), contains useful information in spite of its pro-Portuguese bias.

Several other books paint a vivid picture of the nature of Portuguese rule. Henry W. Nevinson's exposé of Angola in 1903 has recently been reprinted in paperback – *A Modern Slavery* (Schocken Books, 1968). Marvin Harris's pamphlet *Portugal's African Wards* (American Committee on Africa, 1958) describes conditions in Mozambique. The first half of Eduardo Mondlane's *The Struggle for Mozambique* (Penguin Books, 1969) is a critique of Portuguese colonialism in Mozambique by the first President of the Mozambique Liberation Front. A series of articles by Perry Anderson, which appeared first in *New Left Review* (1962), are well worth study for his clear and concise analysis.

Other sources quoted in this chapter are:

Caetano, Marcelo, *Alguns Discursos e Relatórios; Viagem Ministerial a Africa em 1945*, Agência Geral das Colónias, 1946.

Enes, António, *Moçambique; Relatório Apresentado ao Govêrno*. Agência Geral das Colónias, 1946 (1893).

Gilchrist, Sid, *Angola Awake*, The Ryerson Press, 1968.

Mozambique Revolution (periodical bulletin of the Mozambique Liberation Front).

Trend, J. B., *Portugal*, Praeger, 1957.

Chapter 2

There is no good account of the relationship of the United States with Portugal prior to 1960. Most of the studies of American foreign policy, or even of NATO, refer to Portugal, if at all, in a few sentences only. Among the sources that proved of some use are:

Acheson, Dean, *On the Rhodesian Question*, Rhodesian Information Office, 1969.
  Present at the Creation, W. W. Norton, 1969.
Attwood, William, *The Reds and the Blacks*, Harper & Row, 1967.
Berle, Adolf A., Jr, *Tides of Crisis*, Reynal, 1957.
Bowles, Chester, *Africa's Challenge to America*, University of California Press, 1956.
de Figueiredo, Antonio, *Portugal and Its Empire; The Truth*, 1961.
Kennan, George F., *Memoirs; 1925–1950*, Little, Brown, 1967.
Reitzel, William, et al., *United States Foreign Policy; 1945–1955*, The Brookings Institution, 1956.
Roy, Elizabeth C., *United States Military Commitments*, Institute for Defense Analysis, 1963.
Stillman, Calvin W., ed., *Africa in the Modern World*, University of Chicago Press, 1955.
United States in World Affairs, Harper & Row, for the Council on Foreign Relations, annual.
Viner, Jacob, *The American Interest in the 'Colonial Problem'*, Council on Foreign Relations, 1944.
Whitaker, Arthur P., *Spain and the Defense of the West*, Praeger, 1962.

Two recent books useful for understanding the basis of postwar American foreign policy are Gabriel Kolko, *The Roots of American Foreign Policy* (Beacon, 1969), and Harry Magdoff, *The Age of Imperialism* (Monthly Review, 1969).

Chapter 3

Ronald Chilcote, in his book *Portuguese Africa* (Prentice-Hall, 1967) presents a general picture of the development of the nationalist movements in Portuguese Africa. For Guinea-Bissau there are three useful books, one a collection of articles and speeches by Amilcar Cabral, leader of the PAIGC and an important revolutionary theoretician (*Revolution in Guinea*, Stage 1, 1969), and the other two accounts by two journalists who have visited the area of Guinea liberated by

Suggested Reading and Other Sources

PAIGC. Gerard Chaliand's *Armed Struggle in Africa* is published by Monthly Review Press (1969), and Basil Davidson's *The Liberation of Guiné* by Penguin Books (1969). On Angola John Marcum's *The Angolan Revolution* (Volume 1: 1950–1962) (MIT Press, 1969), and Douglas Wheeler and René Pelissier's *Angola*, academic in stance, are the only overall surveys so far in English. A collection of interviews with MPLA cadres by Donald Barnett is due to be published shortly. Two earlier books in French by Robert Davezies (*Les Angolais*, 1965, and *La Guerre d'Angola*, 1968) contain interviews with members of UPA (GRAE) and MPLA. On Mozambique, Eduardo Mondlane's book *The Struggle for Mozambique* (Penguin Books, 1969) is the indispensable source.

Such sources are often rapidly outpaced by the development of the struggle. For current information one should refer to the documents of the movements themselves, many of which are translated or reprinted in English by Liberation Support Movement, Box 338, Richmond, B.C., Canada. Important secondary sources are *Facts and Reports* (bi-weekly press cuttings published by the Angola Comité, Da Costastraat 88, Amsterdam, Holland), and the reports of the United Nations Committee on Decolonization.

Chapter 4

As for the earlier period, there is no one source which analyses American policy towards Portugal during this period, although sections of Marcum's *Angolan Revolution* discuss policy in 1961 and 1962. Sources referred to in the text are as follows:

Acheson, Dean, *Power and Diplomacy*, Harvard University Press, 1958.
Ball, George W., *The Discipline of Power*, Little, Brown, 1968.
Gerberding, William B., *United States Foreign Policy: Perspectives and Analysis*, McGraw-Hill, 1966.
Rivkin, Arnold, *Africa and the West*, Praeger, 1962.
   The African Presence in World Affairs, Free Press, 1963.
Sarmento Rodrigues, M. M., *Presença de Moçambique na Vida da Nação*, Agencia-Geral do Ultramar, 1964–5.
Schlesinger, Arthur, Jr, *A Thousand Days*, Houghton Mifflin, 1965.
Sorenson, Theodore, *Kennedy*, Harper, 1965.
Szulc, Tad, *Dominican Diary*, Delacorte Press, 1965.
United States in World Affairs, Harper & Row, for the Council on Foreign Relations, annual.

Walton, Richard J., *The Remnants of Power*, Coward-McCann, 1968.

Chapter 5

The most important source for further details on the topic of this chapter is the pamphlet *Portugal and Nato*, published by the Angola Comité (Da Costastraat 88, Amsterdam, Holland), and occasional reports from the liberation movements on equipment captured, or on testimony of deserters. The information in this chapter and in Chapter 7 has been obtained primarily from official sources such as Portuguese military journals, and from accounts by observers. The *Portuguese and Colonial Bulletin* (London) covers the Portuguese press, and picks up many interesting items. Current information often appears in the press cuttings reprinted in the Angola Comité's *Facts and Reports*. Also referred to in this chapter are Edgar Cardoso's *Presença da Força Aérea em Angola* (Secretaria de Estado de Aeronáutica, 1963), the official *NATO Handbook* for 1965, and the Abshire and Samuels Handbook mentioned above (Chapter 1).

Chapter 6

There is much information on the economy of Portuguese Africa in Abshire and Samuels, eds, *Portuguese Africa*. The annual reports of the UN Committee on Decolonization are basic sources of current information, as are the quarterly surveys of the Economist Intelligence Unit. As on other topics, much can be gleaned from the *Portuguese and Colonial Bulletin* and *Facts and Reports*. A recent study by Mario de Andrade and Marc Ollivier (*La Guerre en Angola*, Maspero, 1971) examines the effect of the war on the political economy of Angola. More details on Gulf Oil can be found in a pamphlet by the Committee of Returned Volunteers (840 W. Oakdale Ave, Chicago, Illinois 60657) entitled *Gulf Oil; A Study in Exploitation*, and in the July–August 1970 special issue of *Africa Today*. The Hudson Institute study quoted in the text is *Angola; Some Views of Development Prospects* (HI-1278-RR, 13–14 October 1969). Also quoted was *The Terror Fighters* (Purnell, 1969) by South African journalist Al J. Venter.

Suggested Reading and Other Sources

Chapter 7

Most of the information in this chapter is from periodical and pamphlet sources. Those interested in finding out more about the involvement of particular countries should check out the following sources:

On South Africa: Abdul Minty, *South Africa's Defence Strategy*, Anti-Apartheid Movement, London; Al Venter, *The Terror Fighters*, Purnell, 1969; Michael Morris, *Terrorism*, Timmins, 1971; and *Sechaba*, monthly organ of the ANC of South Africa. Venter and Morris are two examples of a genre likely to increase in the future, South African accounts of the war going on in Southern Africa. Read with caution, they may nevertheless be quite revealing.

On Great Britain: See the publications of the Anti-Apartheid Movement and of the Committee for Freedom in Mozambique, Angola, and Guinea-Bissau, as well as *Portuguese and Colonial Bulletin*.

On Germany and France: Refer, first of all, to the publications of the Angola Comité, Holland, especially the pamphlet *Portugal and Nato*.

On Brazil: An important book for background is *Brazil and Africa* by J. H. Rodrigues (University of California Press, 1969).

Chapter 8

On the making of American foreign policy, two basic books, Kolko's *The Roots of American Foreign Policy*, and Magdoff's *The Age of Imperialism*, have already been mentioned. The best discussion to date of the Council on Foreign Relations is in G. William Domhoff, *The Higher Circles* (Random House, 1970). Other books referred to in this chapter are:

Abshire, David and Samuels, Michael, eds., *Portuguese Africa; A Handbook*, Praeger, 1969.

Ball, George, W., *The Discipline of Power*, Little, Brown, 1968.

Nielsen, Waldemar, *African Battleline*, Harper & Row, 1965.

  The Great Powers and Africa, Praeger, 1969.

Williams, G. Mennen, *Africa for the Africans*, Eerdmans, 1969.

Chapters 9 and 10

Among the most important books published recently are Basil Davidson, *In the Eye of the Storm: Angola's People* (Doubleday, 1972) and Don Barnett and Roy Harvey, *The Revolution in Angola: MPLA, Life Histories and Documents* (Bobbs-Merrill, 1972), which give an over-all picture of the struggle in Angola. The authors of both have been inside Angola with MPLA. MPLA has published its own brief account, *Revolution in Angola*, available through Merlin Press in London. Franz Sitte, an Austrian journalist who supports UNITA and considers himself an adventurer, has written an account of a visit inside in *Flammenherd Angola* (Vienna, 1972). Of the three books, Davidson's contains analysis and historical background as well as description.

On Portugal three books published recently give somewhat more background information than has been available before. H. Kay's *Salazar and Modern Portugal* (London: Eyre & Spottiswoode, 1970) is an extensive account by an observer friendly to Salazar. A. H. De Oliveira Marques has written a *History of Portugal* (Columbia University Press, 1972), the second volume of which provides a well-organized account of the modern period. Mário Soares, long-time Portuguese opposition leader, has written a fascinating political autobiography, *Le Portugal Bailloné* (Paris: Calmann-Lévy, 1972).

Also of interest is the chapter on Mozambique in John Saul and Giovanni Arrighi, *Essays on the Political Economy of Africa* (Monthly Review Press, 1973). A pamphlet published by the Angola Comité, with the imposing title *Petition by the Angola Comité Concerning the Report by Mr Pierre Juvigny Regarding the Implementation of the Abolition of Forced Labour Convention, 1957 by Portugal* (1972) is very interesting because it contains the text of a confidential report by a Portuguese colonial official, Dr Afonso Mendes, revealing from within the character of the colonial system.

Index